JEWS WITHOUT MONEY

Jews Without Money

by

Michael Gold

With a Special Introduction
by the Author

woodcuts by Howard Simon

CARROLL & GRAF PUBLISHERS, INC.
New York

TO

LITTLE MIKE

my beloved pest of a nephew,

aged 4,

who helped me write

this book.

First Carroll & Graf edition 1984.

Third Printing 1990

Carroll & Graf Publishers, Inc.
260 Fifth Avenue
New York, N.Y. 10001

ISBN: 0-88184-026-2

Manufactured in the United States of America

INTRODUCTION

A GERMAN friend told me recently in New York about her arrest by the Nazis. It was a week or so after Hitler had taken power and had begun his great lynching party against liberals, radicals and Jews.

The dark ages had returned; modern thought was again burning in the flames of a new inquisition, the Jews again afflicted with the yellow badge of shame.

My friend, a radical, expected a visit from the Brown Shirts, but as calmly as possible continued literary work. It happened that she was translating a chapter from my book, "Jews Without Money," when armed Nazis finally broke in. The officer picked up some sheets of her manuscript, and read, "Jews Without Money."

"Ho, ho, ho!" he roared. "So there are Jews without money!" And all the Brown Shirts laughed with him at the marvelous joke. How could there be Jews without money, when as every good Nazi knew with Hitler, Jews were all international bankers?

Hitler is a demagogue who has falsified history. He succeeds because his followers are too ignorant to know that he lies. The great mass of Jews in the world today are not millionaire bankers, but paupers and workers.

I have told in my book a tale of Jewish poverty in one ghetto, that of New York. The same story can be told of a hundred other ghettoes scattered over all the world. For centuries the Jew has lived in this universal ghetto. Yiddish literature is saturated with the ghetto melancholy and poverty.

And Jewish bankers are fascists everywhere. Hitler has received their support, both with money and ideas. Some of his most important secret conferences were held in the home of a Jewish banker. They gave large sums to his party before he came to power.

Hitler's whole program is to save the banking and profiteering capitalist system. The attack on the Jews is merely a piece of demagogy, to throw the hungry German masses off the trail of their real enemy.

No, every Jew is not a millionaire. The majority of Jews belongs to the working-class and to the bankrupt lower middle class. It is natural that in the present hour so many of them are to be found in the Socialist, Communist and trade union ranks. Jewish bankers are fascists; Jewish workers are radicals; the historic class division is true among the Jews as with any other race.

I was first proud of my book when I visited Germany in 1931 and found that the German radicals had translated it and were spreading it widely as a form of propaganda against the Nazi anti-Semitic lies.

The book has also been translated into French, Swedish, Roumanian, Spanish, Jugo-Slavian, Italian, Japanese, Chinese, Ukrainian, Russian, Yiddish, Bohemian, Bulgarian, Dutch and Tartar.

This means, I hope, that hundreds of thousands of people have perhaps been helped to see that not all Jews are millionaire bankers.

It has become necessary now in America to fight against this great fascist lie. Recently, groups of anti-Semitic demagogues have appeared in this country. They are like Hitler, telling the hungry American people that capitalism is Jewish, and that an attack on the Jews is the best way of restoring prosperity. What folly! What criminal deception and bloody fraud! And there are signs that this oldest of swindles will grow in America.

The defense of the Jewish race against these fascist liars and butchers has become one of the most necessary tasks for every liberal and radical. This is not only a problem for Jews to meet; it has become the problem of the workers and farmers whose hunger the fascists try to appease with the empty husk of anti-Semitism.

My mother, who is the heroine of "Jews Without Money," died just a year ago this month. She lived, to the last, in the same East Side tenement street, and prayed in the same synagogue. This was her world; though her sons born in America were forced into a different world.

We could not worship her gods. But we loved our mother; and she loved us; and the life of this brave and beautiful proletarian woman is the best answer to the fascist liars I know; and it is in the bones of her three sons, and they will never betray their mother, who was a worker and a Jew, nor their race and class, but will honor her dear memory, and fight the fascists in her defense until the bitter end.

MICHAEL GOLD.

New York, April, 1935.

JEWS WITHOUT MONEY

CONTENTS

Chapter 1

FIFTY CENTS A NIGHT

1

I CAN never forget the East Side street where I lived as a boy.

It was a block from the notorious Bowery, a tenement canyon hung with fire-escapes, bed-clothing, and faces.

Always these faces at the tenement windows. The street never failed them. It was an immense excitement. It never slept. It roared like a sea. It exploded like fireworks.

People pushed and wrangled in the street. There were armies of howling pushcart peddlers. Women screamed, dogs barked and copulated. Babies cried.

A parrot cursed. Ragged kids played under truck-horses. Fat housewives fought from stoop to stoop. A beggar sang.

At the livery stable coach drivers lounged on a bench. They hee-hawed with laughter, they guzzled cans of beer.

Pimps, gamblers and red-nosed bums; peanut politicians, pugilists in sweaters; tinhorn sports and tall longshoremen in overalls. An endless pageant of East

Side life passed through the wicker doors of Jake Wolf's saloon.

The saloon goat lay on the sidewalk, and dreamily consumed a *Police Gazette*.

East Side mothers with heroic bosoms pushed their baby carriages, gossiping. Horse cars jingled by. A tinker hammered at brass. Junkbells clanged.

Whirlwinds of dust and newspaper. The prostitutes laughed shrilly. A prophet passed, an old-clothes Jew with a white beard. Kids were dancing around the hurdy-gurdy. Two bums slugged each other.

Excitement, dirt, fighting, chaos! The sound of my street lifted like the blast of a great carnival or catastrophe. The noise was always in my ears. Even in sleep I could hear it; I can hear it now.

2

THE East Side of New York was then the city's red light district, a vast 606 playground under the business management of Tammany Hall.

The Jews had fled from the European pogroms; with prayer, thanksgiving and solemn faith from a new Egypt into a new Promised Land.

They found awaiting them the sweatshops, the bawdy houses and Tammany Hall.

There were hundreds of prostitutes on my street. They occupied vacant stores, they crowded into flats and apartments in all the tenements. The pious Jews hated the traffic. But they were pauper strangers here; they could do nothing. They shrugged their shoulders, and murmured: "This is America." They tried to live.

They tried to shut their eyes. We children did not shut our eyes. We saw and knew.

On sunshiny days the whores sat on chairs along the sidewalks. They sprawled indolently, their legs taking up half the pavements. People stumbled over a gauntlet of whores' meaty legs.

The girls gossiped and chirped like a jungle of parrots. Some knitted shawls and stockings. Others hummed. Others chewed Russian sunflower seeds and monotonously spat out the shells.

The girls winked and jeered, made lascivious gestures at passing males. They pulled at coat-tails and cajoled men with fake honeyed words. They called their wares like pushcart peddlers. At five years I knew what it was they sold.

The girls were naked under flowery kimonos. Chunks of breast and belly occasionally flashed. Slippers hung from their feet; they were always ready for "business."

Earth's trees, grass, flowers could not grow on my street; but the rose of syphilis bloomed by night and by day.

3

IT was a spring morning. I had joined, as on other
mornings, my gang of little Yids gathered on the
sidewalk. There were six or seven of us.

Spring excited us. The sky was blue over our
ghetto. The sidewalks sparkled, the air was fresh.
Everything seemed hopeful. In winter the streets were
vacant, now people sprang up by magic.

Parades of Jews had appeared in these first soft
days, to walk, to talk. To curse, to bargain, to smoke
pipes, to sniff like hibernating bears at the spring.

Pushcarts appeared. Pale bearded peddlers crawled
from their winter cellars, again shouted in the street.
Oranges blazed on the carts; calico was for sale,
clocks, sweet potatoes, herrings, potted geraniums
and goloshes. Spring ushered in a huge, ragged fair.

We spun tops on the sidewalks. We chased street
cars and trucks and stole dangerous rides. Nigger,
our leader, taught us how to steal apples from a
pushcart. We threw a dead cat into the store of the
Chinese laundryman. He came out, a yellow madman,
a hot flat-iron in his hand. We ran away.

Nigger then suggested a new game: that we tease
the prostitutes.

We began with Rosie. She lounged in a tenement
hallway, a homely little woman in a red shawl.
Ready, go. We spurted before ner in short dashes,
our hearts beating with danger and joy.

We screamed at her, making obscene gestures:

"Fifty cents a night! That's what you charge; fifty cents a night! Yah, yah, yah!"

Rosie started. A look came into her sleepy eyes. But she made no answer. She drew her shawl about her. We were disappointed. We had hoped she would rave and curse.

"Fifty cents a night! Fifty cents a night!"

Rosie bit her lip. Spots appeared on her sallow face. That was all; she wouldn't talk. The game didn't work. We tried again. This time she turned on her heel and walked into the gloomy hallway. We looked for another victim.

4

A FAT, haughty prostitute sat on a chair two tenements away. She wore a red kimono decorated with Japanese cherry trees, mountains, waterfalls and old philosophers. Her black hair was fastened by a diamond brooch. At least a million dollars' worth of paste diamonds glittered from her fat fingers.

She was eating an apple. She munched it slowly with the dignity of a whole Chamber of Commerce at its annual banquet. Her lap spread before her like a table.

We scampered around her in a monkey gang. We yelled those words whose terrible meaning we could not fully guess:

"Fifty cents a night!"

Aha. This time the plans of our leader worked. The game was a good one. The fat prostitute purpled with rage. Her eyes bulged with loathing. Sweat appeared on her painted cheeks. She flung her apple at us, and screamed: "Thieves! American bummers! Loafers! Let me catch you! I'll rip you in half!"

She spat like a poisoned cat. She shook her fist. It was fun. The whole street was amused.

"Fifty cents a night! Yah, yah, yah!"

Then I heard my mother's voice calling me from the tenement window. I hated to leave the fun, just when it was good. But my mother called me again and again. So up I went.

I entered blinking from the sunlight. I was surprised to find Rosie sitting in our kitchen. She was crying. My mother pounced upon me and slapped my face.

"Murderer!" she said, "why did you make Rosie cry?"

"Did I make her cry?" I asked stupidly.

My mother grabbed me, and laid me across her knee. She beat me with the cat-o'-nine-tails. I howled and wriggled, but she gave me a good licking. Rosie stood there pleading for me. The poor girl was sorry she had gotten me this licking. My mother was in a rage.

"This will teach you not to play with that Nigger!

This will teach you not to learn all those bad, nasty things in the street!"

Vain beating; the East Side street could not be banished with a leather strap. It was my world; it was my mother's world, too. We *had* to live in it, and learn what it chose to teach us.

5

I WILL always remember that licking, not because it humiliated me, or taught me anything, but because the next day was my fifth birthday.

My father was young then. He loved good times. He took the day off from work and insisted that I be given a birthday party. He bought me a velvet suit with lace collar and cuffs, and patent leather shoes. In the morning he insisted that we all go to be photographed. He made my mother wear her black plush gown. He made her dress my sister in the Scotch plaid. Himself he arrayed in his black suit that made him look like a lawyer.

My mother groaned as we walked through the street. She hated new shoes, new clothes, all fuss or feathers. I was miserable, too. My gang saw me, and snickered at my velvet suit.

But my father was happy, and so was my sister, Esther. They chattered like two children.

It was solemn at the photographer's. My father sat stiffly in a dark carved throne. My mother stood upright beside him, with one hand on his shoulder, to show her wedding ring. My sister rested against my father's knee. I stood on the other side of the throne, holding a basket of artificial flowers.

The bald, eager little photographer disappeared behind a curtain. He snapped his fingers before us, and said, "Watch the birdie." I watched, my neck hurting me because of the clamp. Something clicked; the picture was taken. We went home, exhausted but triumphant.

In the evening the birthday party was held. Many tenement neighbors came with their children. Brandy was drunk, sponge cake and herring eaten, songs were sung. Every one pinched my cheek and praised me. They prophesied I would be a "great man."

Then there was talk. Reb Samuel the umbrella maker was a pious and learned Jew. Whenever he was in a group the talk turned to holy things.

"I have read in the paper," said my father, "that a Dybbuk has entered a girl on Hester Street. But I don't believe it. Are there Dybbuks in America, too?"

"Of course," said Reb Samuel quietly.

Mendel Bum laughed a raucous brandy laugh. He had eaten of everything; the sponge cake, the herring, the quince jam, the apples, *kraut knishes,* fried fish and cheese *blintzes.* He had drunk from every bottle, the fiery Polish *slivovitz,* the *wishniak,* the plum brandy, the Roumanian wine. Now his true nature appeared.

"I don't believe in Dybbuks!" he laughed. "It is all a grandmother story!"

My father banged on the table and leaped to his feet. "Silence, atheist!" he shouted, "in my house we want no wisdom from you!"

Mendel shrugged his shoulders.

"Well," said Reb Samuel quietly, "in the synagogue at Korbin, a girl was once brought. Her lips did not move. From her belly came shrieks and groans of a Dybbuk. He had entered her body while she was in the forest. She was dying with agony.

"The Rabbi studied the matter. Then he instructed two men to take her in a wagon back into that forest. They were told to nail her hair to a tree, drive away with her, and cut off her hair with a scissors.

"This they did. They whipped the horses, and drove and drove. The girl screamed, she raved of fire and water. But when they reached home she was cured. The Dybbuk had left her. All this, my friends, I saw myself."

"Once," said my mother shyly, "I myself saw a Dybbuk that had entered a dog. It was in Hungary. The dog lay under the table and talked in a human voice. Then he gave a long howl and died. So it must be true about the Dybbuks."

6

SOME ONE broke into song. Others marked time with feet and chairs, or beat glasses on the table. When the chorus came, there was a glorious volume of sound. Every one sang, from the venerable Reb Samuel to the smallest child.

My father, that marvelous story-teller, told about a Roumanian ne'er-do-well, who married a grave-digger's daughter that he might succeed to her father's job, and bury all the people who had despised him.

Mottke the vest-maker attacked Jews who changed their names in this country.

"If his name is Garlic in the old country, here he thinks it refined to call himself Mr. Onions," said Mottke.

The mothers talked about their babies. A shy little banana peddler described a Russian pogrom.

"It started at both bazaars, just before the Pass-over," he said. "Some one gave vodka to the peasants, and told them we Jews had killed some Christian children to use the blood. Ach, friends, what one saw then; the yelling, the murder, the flames! I myself saw a peasant cut off my uncle's head with an ax."

At the other end of the table Fyfka the Miser was gobbling all the roast chicken he could grab, and drinking glass after glass of beer. It was a free meal, so he was stuffing himself.

Some one told of a pregnant mother in Russia who had been frightened by a Cossack, and had borne a child with a pig's head.

Leichner the housepainter drank some wine. He told of a Jew in his native village who had been troubled by devils. They were colored red and green and blue. They rattled at the windows every night until the man could get no sleep. He went to a Rabbi and bought six magic words which he repeated until the devils retreated.

The hum of talk, tinkle of glasses, all the hot, happy excitement of the crowded room made me sleepy. I climbed on my mother's lap and began to fall asleep.

"What, too tired even for your own party?" said my mother affectionately.

I heard Reb Samuel talking again in his slow kind voice.

Bang, bang! Two pistol shots rang out in the backyard! I jumped to my feet, with the others. We rushed to the windows. We saw two men with pistols standing in the moonlit yard. Bang, bang! They fired again at each other. One man fell.

The other ran through the hall. A girl screamed in the bawdy house. The clothesline pole creaked. In the moonlight a cat crawled on its belly. It sniffed at the sudden corpse.

"Two gamblers fighting, maybe," said my father.

"Ach, America," Reb Samuel sighed.

All of us left the windows and went back to the singing, and story-telling. It was commonplace, this shooting. The American police would take care of it. It was discussed for some minutes, then forgotten by the birthday party.

But I have never forgotten it, for it burned into my mind the memory of my fifth birthday.

CHAPTER 2

HOW BABIES ARE MADE

1

I REMEMBER another morning in spring. I had always wanted to know what happened inside a whore's room, when she went in with a "customer." That morning Nigger showed me.

One of the girls, Susie, had hailed a truck driver, a giant with red hair. He reined in his horses, climbed from the high seat, and talked to her. Then they went to her room.

Nigger and I followed them. It was on the ground floor of my tenement. Stealthy as detectives, we stared through the keyhole. What I saw made my heart beat, my face redden with shock.

Nigger snickered. He saw I was hurt and it amused him. The couple rose. We sneaked through the hall back to sunlight.

"You got scared," said Nigger.

"No," I said.

"Hell," said Nigger, "every one does it. That's the way babies are made."

"No," I said with unaccountable bitterness. "That's not the way!"

"Yes," said Nigger, "what do you want to bet?"

25

"But that's like saying my mother is like that! You're a liar, Nigger."

Nigger pushed his face close to mine. "I dare you to say that again!" His eyes burned with pugnacity.

"You're a liar! My mother isn't like that!"

Nigger swung at me, and I punched back. In a minute we were a scramble of fists and feet. My gang of little East Siders gathered to watch. They marveled at my courage; Nigger was the tough kid of the gang. But it was not courage; it was the willful suicide of one who has lost his faith.

The battle was swift and one-sided. I was gouged, jabbed, kicked and outpunched. Blood poured from my nose. One eye swelled. At last I ran away. I escaped from the circle of grinning faces. For hours, I brooded by myself in the backyard on a pile of old brick. When it was night I crept up to my home.

My mother scolded me and asked me what had happened. I would not tell her. I could not bear to look in her face. I felt as if she had betrayed me in some way. It took me years to learn that sex can be good as well as evil; more than the thing truck drivers bought for fifty cents on my street.

2

THE worst thing on our street was a certain gang of young loafers. Every East Side street had such a gang at its corners. In the East Side school of crime and poverty these were the apt pupils. They never worked. They played pool all day, or drank in saloons. Some were cheap pimps, others cheap thieves or gunmen. They fought and quarreled with the world, and with each other. There was always a bloody brawl.

They seduced young girls. Every one knew about this. They maintained a flat in one of the tenements. There was no furniture except a dirty old bed. This place was known as the "Camp." Here they brought unsuspecting girls.

It was a kind of sport. I heard them brag about it, and joke. The leader in this fun was Kid Louie. He was a slim dandy. He had been a pugilist, and had a flat nose and cauliflower ear. Many East Side girls thought him handsome. He swaggered. He was a little crazy. He had been pounded so hard in the ring that he was "punch drunk," and could fight no more. His chief pleasure now was to pick up young girls.

He would meet them on the street or at a dance hall and win their friendship. He would bring them up to the "Camp," and pass the signal to others.

"Barlow, just say Barlow to Shorty, Truck, Fat, and the others," he once commanded me. I did not know what it meant. When I said "Barlow" to the gang, their exuberant comments made it clear. I was ashamed of myself. I refused the nickel one of them offered me, and ran away.

Kid Louie would take a girl's clothes from her,

and lock her in the "Camp." Then the other men went
in, one after the other. Sometimes all of them went in
together; this was a "line-up." It is a popular sport
wherever men live in brutal poverty.

One day a tragedy occurred in the "Camp." Kid
Louie took a girl up, and fourteen men attacked her.
An ambulance had to be called. The police looked for
Kid Louie for a week or two. Then everything was for-
gotten. The "Camp" flourished for years.

3

HARRY THE PIMP was not one of these brutes. He had
twenty girls working for him. It was his proud claim
that he had seduced not one of them. He looked upon
himself as a kind of philanthropic business man.
Strangely enough, there were others who regarded him
the same.

Yes, the girls came to him, because he was so wise,
so good and so strong. They begged for his protection.

"They come to me from the gutter," he explained
to an admiring saloon friend. "They are lousy, and
I bathe them. They are hungry; I give them food, and
clothes. I teach them manners, I teach them to be sober
and to save their money. I make something out of
them. Many of my girls have saved enough to bring
their parents from the old country. Many of them
have married wealthy men. I tell you, they are grateful to me. When I tell a girl I won't have anything

to do with her, she cries, and wants to kill herself.

"I never beat my women. I don't need to; they know my value too well. A word from me is sufficient."

Harry was considered handsome. He was pleasingly fat and shiny, and had a curly mustache. He wore good clothes, clean linen, and smoked good cigars. He was mellow, conservative and fatherly. Next to Jake Wolf, the saloonkeeper, he was our pattern of American success. People envied him. He had a big pull with Tammany Hall. He owned a gambling house, and spoke perfect English.

His favorite advice to the young and unsuccessful was to learn English.

"America is a wonderful country," Harry would say, "really a wonderful country. One can make much money here, but first one must learn to speak English.

"That is what I am always preaching to our Jews; learn English; become an American. Is it any wonder you must go on slaving in the sweatshops? Look at me; if I hadn't learned English I myself would still be buried in a shop. But I struggled—I fought—I learned English."

It was Harry the Pimp who gave me my first book to read. "Here, study English," he said. It was a book of fairy-tales, and my sister Esther stole it, of course, and I had to fight her to get it back.

Harry had a wife and two children, of whom he

was very proud. He showed the whores pictures of his
children to be admired. Harry spent part of the day
on our street, but every evening he walked home
solemnly to supper. His family waited every night
for their poppa to come from business: I am sure
they were proud of him.

4

MY parents hated all this filth. But it was America,
one had to accept it. And these were our neighbors.
It's impossible to live in a tenement without being
mixed up with the tragedies and cockroaches of one's
neighbors. There's no privacy in a tenement. So there
was always some girl or other in our kitchen, pouring
out a tale of wretchedness to my mother, drinking tea
and warming herself at my mother's wonderful heart.
That's how I came to know some of the stories of these
girls.

Most of the girls were simple people. They were
like peasants who have been drafted into an army.
They lived in the slime and horror of the trenches,
knowing why as little as soldiers. They made the best
of it.

They were crazy about children, and petted us and
gave us nickels. Some of them loved their pimps with
a dog's devotion. They thought it a privilege to visit
my mother, and to drink tea in a decent home. They
brought my mother presents, to her embarrassment.

My mother disapproved of their life, and told them so with her usual frankness. But she was too kind-hearted to keep them out.

Susie worshiped my mother. She was the prettiest girl on the street, vivid and slim, with the dark fanatic beauty of a prophet's daughter. She had gay little gestures, and was affectionate and unselfish. She should have been popular, but was the most hated girl on the street.

She was always drunk. She made scenes; she fought with all her men, and abused them and cursed them. Her pimp beat her often. She had no friends.

After one of her scenes, she would rush into our kitchen hysterically. She'd throw herself on my mother's shoulder, and passionately kiss her hands.

"Momma, momma, please be kind to me!" she wept. "Tell me what to do, tell me how to save myself!"

"Leave this business," my mother said patiently. "Get a job in a factory, and be a good girl."

"Yes, yes, yes," the girl wept. "I'll do it to-morrow morning, momma." But she never did. My mother tired of these hysterical scenes. She tried to shake Susie off, she acted coldly to her.

One night as we sat at supper we heard groans outside. My father opened the door, and there lay Susie, writhing like a cut worm. She had taken carbolic acid.

"See, momma," she gasped. "I am getting out of the business at last." The ambulance came for her, and she died the next day in the hospital.

5

IDA was an exception. She was one of the Madams, and ran an establishment. She had hired an empty store, and put up curtains to screen the windows. Then ten cubicles were built with beaverboard. A cot was placed in each cubicle, and the store was ready for trade.

Ida was hard-boiled. She was big, fat, aggressive; she wore a big diamond ring and knew how to make money. She liked to drink bucket after bucket of beer. Foaming with beer, she'd brag about the tenement houses she owned, and her youthful prowess as a whore. She bragged that once she had taken on sixty men in a day.

She despised the weak little girls, who worried, and had romantic scruples, and remembered their fathers and mothers.

Masha was one of her girls. Masha was a Russian-Jewish girl who was blind. She had lost her eyes and her family in a Russian pogrom. How she had drifted into the "business" no one ever learned. She had a meek face, and was always quiet. She played songs of Kiev, and accompanied herself on a seven-string guitar. The other girls liked her. But they teased her

about a certain incident, when they had nicknamed
her "Sweetheart of the Yellow Cholera." It was when
a Chinese laundryman had stayed with her. He had
come in drunk, wanting a girl. All the girls refused
him, because of his race. He insisted. For a joke, the
girls sent him into Masha's cubicle. She was blind,
and didn't know the difference.

So they made a great lot of fun of it afterward.
They called her "Sweetheart of the Yellow Cholera."

Many nights I fell asleep to the melodies of Kiev
she sang to her seven-string guitar. We could hear it
in our home. She sang between "customers."

6

THE pimps were hunters. A pretty girl growing up on
the East Side was marked by them. They watched her
fill out, grow tall, take on the sex bloom. When she
was fifteen, they schemed to trap her. They ruined
Nigger's sister when she was fifteen. Louis One Eye
did it.

Pimps infested the dance halls. Here they picked
up the romantic factory girls who came after the
day's work. They were smooth story-tellers. They
seduced the girls the way a child is helped to fall
asleep, with tales of magic happiness.

No wonder East Side parents wouldn't let their
daughters go to dance halls. But girls need to dance.

I have never heard of a millionaire's daughter who

became a fifty-cent whore, or who was "ruined" by dance halls.

7

MANY of the whores were girls who had been starved into this profession. Once in, they knew no way out. They were afraid of starving again if they left.

Rosie worked for years in the sweatshops, saving money to bring her parents from Europe. Then she fell sick. Her savings melted. She went to a hospital. She came out, and could not find a job. She was hungry, feeble, and alone. No one cared whether she lived or died.

She was ready for the river. A pimp met her. He took her to a restaurant, and fed her her first solid meal. He made her a practical offer. Rosie accepted. She never regretted her choice; it was easier than being in a sweatshop. She saved money to send to her parents, and was never sick with asthma again.

Thus Tammany Hall grew rich. Our landlord, Mr. Zunzer, grew rich. My mother once complained to him about some whores who held noisy drunken parties late at night.

Mr. Zunzer was a pillar of the synagogue. He wore a long frock coat spotted with grease, and a white boiled shirt, but no collar or necktie.

"Yes," he said, stroking his bushy beard, "those girls are whores. But they pay three times the rent you do, and they pay promptly. So if you want to move out, please do so. A black year on it, but a landlord must live!"

All these things happened. They were part of our daily lives, not lurid articles in a Sunday newspaper.

CHAPTER 3

A GANG OF LITTLE YIDS

1

I FIRST admired Nigger in school, when I was new there. He banged the teacher on the nose.

School is a jail for children. One's crime is youth, and the jailers punish one for it. I hated school at first; I missed the street. It made me nervous to sit stiffly in a room while New York blazed with autumn.

I was always in hot water. The fat old maid teacher (weight about 250 pounds), with a sniffle, and eyeglasses, and the waddle of a ruptured person, was my enemy.

She was shocked by the dirty word I, a six-year-old villain, once used. She washed my mouth with yellow lye soap. I submitted. She stood me in the corner for the day to serve as an example of anarchy to a class of fifty scared kids.

Soap eating is nasty. But my parents objected because soap is made of Christian fat, is not kosher. I was being forced into pork-eating, a crime against the Mosaic law. They complained to the Principal.

O irritable, starched old maid teacher, O stupid, proper, unimaginative despot, O cow with no milk or calf or bull, it was torture to you, Ku Kluxer before your time, to teach in a Jewish neighborhood.

I knew no English when handed to you. I was a little savage and lover of the street. I used no toothbrush. I slept in my underwear, I was lousy, maybe. To sit on a bench made me restless, my body hated coffins. But Teacher! O Teacher for little slaves, O ruptured American virgin of fifty-five, you should not have called me "LITTLE KIKE."

Nigger banged you on the nose for that. I should have been as brave. It was Justice.

2

KU KLUX moralizers say the gangster system is not American. They say it was brought here by "low-class" European immigrants. What nonsense! There never were any Jewish gangsters in Europe. The Jews there were a timid bookish lot. The Jews have done no killing since Jerusalem fell. That's why the murder-loving Christians have called us the "peculiar people." But it is America that has taught the sons of tubercular Jewish tailors how to kill.

Nigger was a virile boy, the best pitcher, fighter and crapshooter in my gang. He was George Washington when our army annihilated the redcoats. He rode the mustangs, and shot the most buffalo among the tenements. He scalped Indians, and was our stern General in war.

Some of the gang have become famous. Al Levy was known to us simply as "Stinker"; now he writes wealthy musical comedies.

Abe Sugarman is a proud movie director. He also has become a Spanish nobleman. His Hollywood name is Arturo De Sagaar, no less.

Lew Moses shoots craps with high stakes, with skyscrapers; he is a big real estate speculator.

Others of the boys are humbler comedians. Jake Gottlieb is a taxi driver, and feeds his three kids every day. Harry Weintraub is a clothing cutter. Some of the boys are dead.

There was always something for boys to see in the free enormous circus of the East Side. Always a funeral, a riot, a quarrel between two fat mommas, or an accident, or wedding. Day after day we explored the streets, we wandered in this remarkable dream of a million Jews.

Our gang played the universal games, tag, prisoner's base, duck on a rock. Like boys in Africa and Peru, we followed the seasons religiously for kites, tops and marbles.

One of the most exciting games was invented by Nigger. It was the stealing game. Nigger ran the fastest, so he would march up to a pushcart and boldly steal a piece of fruit. The outraged peddler chased him, of course, which was the signal for us to grab fruit and run the other way.

With a penny one could buy much; a hot dog, or a cup of cocoa, or one of thirty varieties of poisoned candies. Watermelon, apples, and old world delicacies like Turkish *halvah* and *lakoom; liver knishes;* Russian sunflower seeds; Roumanian pastry; pickled tomatoes. For a nickel a mixture of five of these street luxuries produced amazing Jewish nightmares.

We turned on the fire hydrant in summer, and splashed in the street, shoes, clothes and all. Or went swimming from the docks. Our East River is a sunspangled open sewer running with oily scum and garbage. It should be underground, like a sewer. It stinks with the many deaths of New York. Often while swimming I had to push dead swollen dogs and vegetables from my face. In our set it was considered humor to slyly paddle ordure at another boy when he was swimming.

What a dirty way of getting clean. But the sun was shining, the tugboats passed, puffing like bulldogs, the freight boats passed, their pale stokers hanging over the rails, looking at us, the river flowed and glittered, the sky was blue, it was all good.

Nigger taught us how to swim. His method was to throw a boy from the steep pier. If the boy swam, well and good. If he sank and screamed for help, Nigger laughed and rescued him.

Jack Korbin died that way, I almost drowned, too.

But it was good. We were naked, free and coocoo

with youngness. Anything done in the sun is good.
The sun, the jolly old sun who is every one's poppa,
looked down as affectionately on his little riffraff
Yids as he did on his syphilitic millionaires at Palm
Beach, I am sure.

3

LET me tell of a trait we boys showed: the hunger for
country things.

New York is a devil's dream, the most urbanized
city in the world. It is all geometry angles and stone.
It is mythical, a city buried by a volcano. No grass
is found in this petrified city, no big living trees, no
flowers, no bird but the drab little lecherous sparrow,
no soil, loam, earth; fresh earth to smell, earth to
walk on, to roll on, and love like a woman.

Just stone. It is the ruins of Pompeii, except that
seven million animals full of earth-love must dwell
in the dead lava streets.

Each week at public school there was an hour called
Nature Study. The old maid teacher fetched from a
dark closet a collection of banal objects: birdnests,
cornstalks, minerals, autumn leaves and other poor
withered corpses. On these she lectured tediously, and
bade us admire Nature.

What an insult. We twisted on our benches, and
ached for the outdoors. It was as if a starving bum
were offered snapshots of food, and expected to feel

grateful. It was like lecturing a cage of young monkeys on the jungle joys.

"Lady, gimme a flower! Gimme a flower! Me, me, me!"

In summer, if a slummer or settlement house lady walked on our street with flowers in her hand, we attacked her, begging for the flowers. We rioted and yelled, yanked at her skirt, and frightened her to the point of hysteria.

Once Jake Gottlieb and I discovered grass struggling between the sidewalk cracks near the livery stable. We were amazed by this miracle. We guarded this treasure, allowed no one to step on it. Every hour the gang studied "our" grass, to try to catch it growing. It died, of course, after a few days; only children are hardy enough to grow on the East Side.

The Italians raised red and pink geraniums in tomato cans. The Jews could have, too, but hadn't the desire. When an excavation was being dug for a new tenement, the Italians swarmed there with pots, hungry for the new earth. Some of them grew bean vines and morning glories.

America is so rich and fat, because it has eaten the tragedy of millions of immigrants.

To understand this, you should have seen at twilight, after the day's work, one of our pick and shovel wops watering his can of beloved flowers. Brown peasant, son of thirty generations of peasants, in a sweaty undershirt by a tenement window, feeling the lost poetry. Uprooted! Lost! Betrayed!

A white butterfly once blundered into our street. We chased it, and Joey Cohen caught it under his cap. But when he lifted the cap, the butterfly was dead. Joey felt bad about this for days.

4

To come back to Nigger.

He was built for power like a tugboat, squat and solid. His eyes, even then, had the contemptuous glare of the criminal and genius. His nose had been squashed at birth, and with his black hair and murky face, made inevitable the East Side nickname: "Nigger."

He was bold, tameless, untouchable, like a little gypsy. He was always in motion, planning mischief. He was suspicious like a cat, quick to sidestep every sudden kick from his enemy, the world. The East Side breeds this wariness. East Side prize fighters have always been of the lightning type; they learn to move fast dodging cops and street cars.

The East Side, for children, was a world plunged in eternal war. It was suicide to walk into the next block. Each block was a separate nation, and when a strange boy appeared, the patriots swarmed.

"What streeter?" was demanded, furiously.

"Chrystie Street," was the trembling reply.

Bang! This was the signal for a mass assault on the unlucky foreigner, with sticks, stones, fists and feet. The beating was cruel and bloody as that of grown-ups, no mercy was shown. I have had three holes in my head, and many black eyes and puffed lips from our street wars. We did it to others, they did it to us. It was patriotism, though what difference there was between one East Side block and another is now hard to see. Each was the same theosophist's fantasy of tenements, demons, old hats, Jews, pushcarts, angels, urine smells, shadows, featherbeds and bananas. The same gray lava streets.

One had to join a gang in self-protection, and be loyal. And one had to be brave. Even I was brave, an odd child cursed with introspection.

Joey Cohen, a dreamy boy with spectacles, was brave. Stinker claimed to be brave, and Jake Gottlieb was brave, and Abie, Izzy, Fat, Maxie, Pishteppel, Harry, all were indubitably brave. We often boasted about our remarkable bravery to each other. But Nigger was bravest of the brave, the chieftain of our brave savage tribe.

Nigger would fight boys twice his age, he would fight men and cops. He put his head down and tore in with flying arms, face bloody, eyes puffed by punching, lips curled back from the teeth, a snarling iron machine, an animal bred for centuries to fighting, yet his father was a meek sick little tailor.

Nigger began to hate cops at an early age. The cops on our street were no worse than most cops, and no better. They loafed around the saloon backdoors, guzzling free beer. They were intimate with the prostitutes, and with all the thieves, cokefiends, pimps and gamblers of the neighborhood. They took graft everywhere, even from the humblest shoelace peddler.

Every one knew what cops were like. Why, then, did they adopt such an attitude of stern virtue toward the small boys? It was as if we were the biggest criminals of the region. They broke up our baseball games, confiscated our bats. They beat us for splashing under the fire hydrant. They cursed us, growled and chased us for any reason. They hated to see us having fun.

We were absorbed in a crap game one day. Suddenly Fat yelled: "Cheese it, the cop!" Every one scattered like rabbits, leaving around 15 pennies on the sidewalk. The cops usually pocketed this small change. It was one of our grievances. We often suspected them of being moralists for the sake of this petty graft.

Nigger didn't run. He bent down calmly and picked up the pennies. He was defying the cop. The cop swelled up like a turkey with purple rage. He slammed Nigger with his club across the spine. Nigger was knocked to the sidewalk. The cop forced the pennies out of Nigger's hand.

"Yuh little bastard," said the cop, "I'll ship yuh to the reformatory yet!"

Nigger stood up quietly, and walked away. His face was hard. Five minutes later a brick dropped from the sky and just missed the cop's skull.

It was Nigger's grim reply. The cop rushed up to the roof, and chased Nigger. But Nigger was too daring to be caught. He leaped gaps between the tenements like a mountain goat. He was ready to die for justice. The cop was not as brave.

For months Nigger remembered to drop bricks, bundles of garbage and paper bags filled with water on this cop's head. It drove the man crazy. But he could never catch the somber little ghost. But he spread the word that Nigger was a bad egg, due for the reformatory. This cop's name was Murph. It was he who later tipped the balances that swung Nigger into his career of gangster.

5

Delancey Street was being torn up to be converted into Schiff Parkway, and there were acres of empty lots there.

On our East Side, suffocated with miles of tenements, an open space was a fairy-tale gift to children.

Air, space, weeds, elbow room, one sickened for space on the East Side, any kind of marsh or wasteland to testify that the world was still young, and wild and free.

My gang seized upon one of these Delancey Street lots, and turned it, with the power of imagination, into a vast western plain.

We buried pirate treasure there, and built snow forts. We played football and baseball through the long beautiful days. We dug caves, and with Peary explored the North Pole. We camped there at night under the stars, roasting sweet potatoes that were sweeter because stolen.

It was there I vomited over my first tobacco, and first marveled at the profundities of sex. It was there I first came to look at the sky.

The elevated train anger was not heard there. The shouting of peddlers like an idiot asylum, the East Side danger and traffic rumble and pain, all were shut by a magic fence out of this boy's Nirvana.

Shabby old ground, ripped like a battlefield by workers' picks and shovels, little garbage dump lying forgotten in the midst of tall tenements, O home of all the twisted junk, rusty baby carriages, lumber, bottles, boxes, moldy pants and dead cats of the neighborhood—every one spat and held the nostrils when passing you. But in my mind you still blaze in a halo of childish romance. No place will ever seem as wonderful again.

We had to defend our playground by force of arms. This made it even more romantic.

One April day, Abie, Jakie, Stinker and I were playing tipcat under the blue sky. The air was warm. Yellow mutts moved dreamily on the garbage. The sun covered the tenements with gold. Pools of melted snow shone in the mud. An old man smoked his pipe and watched us.

Boys feel the moments of beauty, but can't express them except through a crazy exuberance. We were happy. Suddenly a bomb shattered the peace.

The Forsythe Street boys, our enemies, whooped down like a band of Indians. They were led by Butch, that dark fearless boy whose "rep" was formidable as Nigger's.

They proceeded to massacre us. There were about fifteen of them. Abie and Jake were buried under a football pyramid of arms and legs. Stinker, who had earned his nickname because he would whine, beg, weep and stool-pigeon his way out of any bad mess, howled for mercy. Butch worked on me. It was a duel between a cockroach and a subway train.

At last they permitted us to get to our feet.

"Listen, you guys," said Butch, sneering as he wiped his hands on his seat, "this dump belongs to us Forsythe streeters, see? Get the hell out."

We ran off, glad to escape alive. Our shirts were torn, our stockings chewed off, we were muddy and

wounded and in disgrace. We found Nigger. He was
loaded with an immense bundle of men's coats which
he was bringing to his family from the factory. His
family worked at home, this was his daily chore.

He turned pale with rage when he heard of the
massacre. All that afternoon strategy was discussed.
We spied on the Forsythe streeters, we visited the
Eldridge streeters and formed an alliance against the
common enemy.

The very next day the historic battle was fought.
Some of our boys stole tops of washboilers at home,
and used them as shields. Others had tin swords,
sticks, blackjacks. The two armies slaughtered each
other in the street. Bottles were thrown, heads cut
open. Nigger was bravest of the brave.

We won back our playground. And after that we
posted sentries, and enjoyed passwords, drills, and
other military ritual. The old maid teachers would
have been horrified to see us practice their principal
teaching: War. War.

6

BUT the Schiff Parkway was an opponent we could
not defeat. It robbed us of our playground at last.

A long concrete patch was laid out, with anemic
trees and lines of benches where jobless workers sit
in summer.

We went back to our crowded street. Joey Cohen

was killed by the horse car not long afterward.

He had stolen a ride, and in jumping, fell under the wheels. The people around saw the flash of his body, and then heard a last scream of pain.

The car rolled on. The people rushed to the tracks and picked up the broken body of my playmate.

O what a horrible joke happened. The head was missing. Policemen arrived, Joey's father and mother screamed and moaned, every one searched, but the head could not be found.

Later it was discovered under the car, hanging from the bloody axle.

Our gang was depressed by this accident. Jake Gottlieb said he would never steal another ride on a horse car. But Nigger, to show how brave he was, stole a ride that very afternoon.

Joey was the dreamy boy in spectacles who was so sorry when he killed the butterfly. He was always reading books, and had many queer ideas. It was he who put the notion in my head of becoming a doctor. I had always imagined I wanted to be a fireman.

~~~~~~

CHAPTER 4

SUMMER TOADSTOOLS

1

JOEY COHEN! you who were sacrificed under the wheels of a horse car, I see you again, Joey! I see your pale face, so sensitive despite its childish grime and bruises. You are precocious in the Jewish way, full of a strange kindness and understanding. There are dark rings under your eyes, as under mine —we sleep very little in summer. But morning is here, and, Joey, your father gave you a whole nickel. Together we set out to spend it.

We are in bare feet. The pavement blisters us, but we like this fierce contact, and dare each other to walk over the hottest places. We wear no caps. Our heads are shaved, to help our mommas fight the summer lice.

Joey is in cotton undershirt and pants supported by one suspender and a safety pin. Myself about the same.

First we buy two lollipops, a red and a green, at the candy stall on the corner. We suck prodigiously, and sometimes exchange sucks as we loaf and watch the happy dancers around a hand-organ.

My sister Esther is dancing with Nigger's sister

Lily. The sun blazes. The street roars. My sister's face is flushed with joy. In her ecstasy she does not see me. Her pigtails fly, as she jogs in and out the mazes of a Morris dance. There are other dark little skinny girls. Their little bodies are aflame with rhythm. They have followed the hand-organ from street to street, but after hours of dancing are still unsated. Only the Italian organ grinder seems glum and bored. He grinds out a gay two-step as if he were in a factory and holds up his cap for pennies.

That's all he cares about. But the dancers make every one else happy. Some of the prostitutes have left their "business" for a moment, and watch with gentle smiles. The cop leans against a lamppost and smiles. A grim old graybeard with a live chicken under his arm is smiling at the children. A truckdriver has slowed down and watches them dreamily as he rattles by. Mothers watch from the tenement windows. A fat important little business Jew, bursting like a plum with heat, mops his face, and admires the children.

A humpbacked old witch in a red kerchief hobbles by, pushing a baby carriage covered with cloth. There is no baby in there, but a big pot full of hot black-eyed beans.

"*Bubkes!*" she wails in a sort of Chinese falsetto, "buy my hot, fresh *bubkes!*"

We forget the dancing, and remember the pennies

burning a hole in Joey's pocket. We order some *bubkes*. The old wart-faced crone lifts the cloth, she measures a penny's worth of the beans into a paper poke.

As we eat, Joey is thinking. Only two pennies are now left, and they must be spent wisely.

"Let's go to Cheap Haber's!" he says. This is a candy store on Rivington Street, famous for miles among the East Side kids for its splendid bargains. So we mooch along there on one of our adventures of a summer day.

2

I LIKE the summer. So much happens then. Winter is fun, too, with its snowball fights, but summer is a big circus. Yes, then everything happens. Winter is mostly spent indoors. Summer one lives in the street.

Jake Wolf is standing in front of his saloon. He picks his magnificent gold teeth that every one admires so much, and curls his mustache. His white vest sparkles in the sunshine. Jake is a great man. He belongs to Tammany Hall and runs the elections every year.

"Hello, Jake!"

"Hello, kids!"

"Can we have some pretzels, Jake?"

"We're going to Cheap Haber's, Jake."

"That's good. Look out for the Indians."

"Aw, there's no Indians in New York, Jake. Can

we have a pretzel? Tell us about the time you killed that Indian out west."

"Some other time. Run along, boys."

We leave him reluctantly; the great man is kind to boys, generous with free lunch pretzels, and full of fine stories. He spent a year in the west, in Chicago, and saw the Indians. They looked like Jews, he said, but were not as smart or as brave. One Jew could kill a hundred Indians.

A bum was suddenly bounced out of the saloon. He did a funny somersault, and fell on his face, scraping the hard pavement. His cheek gushed with blood; he cursed and groaned. Jake Wolf looked down at the bundle of bloody rags, picked his teeth, spat, yawned and turned away.

"Beat it, boys!" he smiled, winking genially at us, "I'm busy."

3

THERE were many bums in the milk and butter store. They flocked there every morning to drink buttermilk at five cents the quart. Iced buttermilk soothed their inflamed stomachs after a long drunk. Mary Sugar Bum told me that in one of her lucid moments.

On the bench in front of the livery stable the drivers were having a load of fun. They were feeding beer out of a can to Terry McGovern the goat.

Most saloons had mascots. Terry was the mascot for Jake's saloon. He was a big dirty mean he-goat

named after Terry McGovern the prize fighter. His
horns were gilded, and he wore a large dog-collar
studded with brass knobs. His name was engraved on
the collar, and the address of Jake's saloon. Terry
lived on free lunch, and garbage, newspapers, tin
cans, any old thing. His eating habits were the talk of
the neighborhood. And he also was crazy about beer.
He lapped it up like a thirsty bum who has just pan-
handled a nickel on a hot day. Then he frisked his
tail, and butted everything in sight. It was great fun.
The drivers spent many dimes buying beer for Terry.

Once I saw a drunken sailor lie down on the sidewalk and butt heads with Terry. What a damn fool.
The goat cracked the sailor's head open, and an ambulance had to be called.

4

THE summer! A fire engine screamed by on the next
street. It cut through the traffic like a cannonball going through a regiment of soldiers. Then, what excitement, an ambulance a minute later. It forced wagons,
pushcarts, men, women and children, to scatter like
rats. Joey Cohen and I debated: which was the most
heroic career: fireman or doctor?

We saw a scissors grinder. He was an old German
with silky white whiskers and eyeglasses. He looked
like a doctor, so neat and dignified. He rang a bell,
and pushed his grindstone on its big cartwheel. He

went into a butcher shop, and came out with an armful
of knives and cleavers. We watched the golden sparks
fly.

Then a big sightseeing bus rolled down. A gang of
kids chased it, and pelted rocks, garbage, dead cats
and stale vegetables at the frightened sightseers.
"Liars, liars"; the kids yelled, "go back up-town!"
Joey and I joined in the sport. What right had these
stuckup foreigners to come and look at us? What
right had that man with the megaphone to tell them
lies about us? Kids always pelted these busses. The
sport is still popular on the East Side.

5

How many temptations beset us. How often Joey and
I stopped to debate whether to spend the money now or
to march on to Cheap Haber's. But we were strong
and went on.

Temptations. There was the mysterious lemonade
man. He appeared each summer, a swarthy bandit
with fierce pointed mustaches. He wore a Turkish fez,
white balloon pants, and a red sash. On his back hung
a brass kettle with a long graceful spout. For a penny
he bowed to the pavement as if in prayer. From the
spout over his shoulder Turkish lemonade poured into
the glass in his hand. It was a splendid performance,
worth a penny to command.

And we met a merry-go-round, a little one with six

wooden steeds mounted on a wagon and pulled by an old horse. The man in charge turned a wheel and made the kids spin until they were dizzy. The man was small, dark and broad as a beer-keg. He was a Jew, but looked like an Italian. He hated kids. The ones who had had rides but still lingered he drove off with his whip.

We saw a fortune-teller with a hand-organ and a parrot. The parrot and the man had big noses. For a penny, the parrot picked a printed slip out of a box and gave it to you. It told you your fortune.

6

THIS was summer. An old melancholy Jew limped by, with six derby hats stacked one over the other on his head, and a burlap sack on his shoulder.

"I Cash Clothes!" he wailed, gazing with weary eyes up and down the tenement walls. "I Cash Clothes!" and it made one's heart ache strangely, like the synagogue prayers at Yom Kippur.

In my ears still ring the lamentations of the lonely old Jews without money:

"I cash clothes, I cash clothes, my God, why hast Thou forsaken me?"

7

SUMMER. Everywhere the garbage. Plop, bung, and another fat, spreading bundle dropped from a tene-

ment window. Many of the East Side women had this horrible custom. To save walking downstairs, they wrapped their garbage in newspapers and flung it in the street. In summer the East Side heavens rained with potato peelings, coffee grounds, herring heads and dangerous soup bones. Bang, went a bundle, and the people in the street ducked as if a machine gun sounded.

Summer heat. The asphalt bubbled underfoot. The horses pulled their hoofs with a loud sucking noise out of boiling tar streets. One's own bare feet sank in the tar, and left a deep print.

Joey and I saw an old lady sitting on a stoop, surrounded by people. They had taken off her corset and orthodox wig, and were fanning her. They offered her cold soda water to drink. She was sunstruck.

Flies, bedbugs, sick cats, sunstruck horses, men and women, and busy saloons, and street circus— Summer.

In the maelstrom of wagons, men, pushcarts, street cars, dogs and East Side garbage, the mothers calmly wheeled their baby carriages. They stopped in the shade of the Elevated trains, to suckle their babies with big sweaty breasts.

Summer's morning! Joey Cohen and I walking to Cheap Haber's!

8

WE never got there. A summer nightmare intervened.
At Chrystie and Rivington streets, opposite the Mills
Hotel, a man called to us from a doorway. I did not
like him from the start. He was a bum in moldy,
wrinkled clothes saturated like a foul kitchenrag with
grease. His knees showed through the pants, and he
was spotted with the sawdust of some saloon floor.
His rusty yellow face was covered with sores. He was
gruesome. He was like a corpse in the first week of
decomposition.

His hands twitched and bulged in his pockets. His
eyes were bright as a rat's, and blinked incessantly.

"Come here!" croaked this scarecrow, "do you want
to earn a nickel?"

I was frightened. The man's bruised mouth slobbered, and I feared his pinpoint eyes. But a nickel
tempted Joey. He was braver than I. He went over to
talk with the man.

The man took him into the tenement hallway.

I waited in the street. A minute or two passed, but
it seemed longer. I fidgeted nervously. An old bearded
Jew peddling apples read a newspaper serenely by
his pushcart. I stood beside him and looked at the
apples.

Suddenly I heard a scream. Joey rushed out of the
tenement pursued by the scarecrow corpse.

"Momma, momma!" Joey screamed. "He tried to take my pants off!"

The old peddler stood up, his glasses falling down his nose in amazement. Joey flung himself into the old man's arms. The scarecrow, grinding his teeth and making queer strangled noises, knocked the old peddler to the sidewalk. He grabbed Joey. What eyes. They bulged, red and swollen, from the sockets. The eyelids flapped frantically.

Joey fought and screamed. The man held him. Suddenly a fat, snubnosed little Jew in flannel shirt and cap appeared. He was smoking a pipe. He took it out of his mouth, and swung two powerful blows at the corpse's jaw.

"You goddamned pervert, let that kid go!" said the stout little man. The bum was staggered by the punches. He released Joey, and looked around him wildly. Other people had gathered. A knife flashed. Blood spurted from a red, crooked line. The pervert had slashed the face of the stout little man. It was all swift as lightning.

Two Italian laborers had been digging a sewer nearby. They were electrified with rage. They swung their shovels over their heads, and crashed them down on the bum's skull. He collapsed to the sidewalk with a gasp. And then an epidemic of madness swept the sudden crowd. Bedlam, curses, blood, a tornado of inflamed cruel faces. Every one, even the women,

kicked, punched, and beat with shovels the limp ugly
body on the sidewalk. One told the other what this
man had done. It turned people insane. If a cop had
not arrived, the pervert would have been torn into
little bleeding hunks.

Joey and I, forgotten, escaped from this scene.
Joey was sobbing bitterly, and I did not know what
to do for him. Neither of us now had the slightest desire to go to Cheap Haber's or to find any other adventures that morning. We wanted to be back on our
own block. We broke into a trot, Joey gulping with
sobs as he ran.

And then, at last, we arrived in safety at our own
block. And there the little girls were still dancing
around the hand-organ with such joy. The grown-ups
still watched them with caressing smiles. Their world
was still the same, though ours had forever changed.
Never would Joey or I quite trust a stranger again.
Never would we walk without fear through the East
Side. Now we knew it as a jungle, where wild beasts
prowled, and toadstools grew in a poisoned soil—per-
verts, cokefiends, kidnapers, firebugs, Jack the
Rippers.

CHAPTER 5

DID GOD MAKE BEDBUGS?

1

IT rained, we squatted dull as frogs on the steps of the rear tenement. What boredom in the backyard, we kids didn't know what to do. Life seemed to flicker out on a rainy day.

The rain was warm and sticky; it spattered on the tin roofs like a gangster's blood. It filled our backyard with a smell of decay, as if some one had dumped a ton of rotten apples.

Rain, rain! The sky was a strip of gray tin above the terraced clotheslines, on which flowery shirts and underwear flapped in the rain. I looked up at them.

I heard the hum of sewing machines, surf on a desolate island. A baby wept feebly. Its hoarse mother answered. The swollen upper half of a fat woman hung from a window, her elbows like hams. She stared with dull eyes at the rain.

A wooden shack occupied a portion of the yard; it was the toilet. A bearded man in suspenders went in.

Masha sang from the next tenement. The deep Russian songs helped her pain, the blind girl was homesick. Others girls sang with her often, many nights

I fell asleep to that lullaby. Now she sang alone.

Because there was nothing to do. Rain, rain, we had tired of our marbles, our dice and our playing store games.

The backyard was a curious spot. It had once been a graveyard. Some of the old American headstones had been used to pave our Jewish yard. The inscriptions were dated a hundred years ago. But we had read them all, we were tired of weaving romances around these ruins of America.

Once we had torn up a white gravestone. What an adventure. We scratched like ghouls with our hands deep into the earth until we found moldy dirty human bones. What a thrill that was. I owned chunks of knee bone, and yellow forearms, and parts of a worm-eaten skull. I had them cached in a secret corner of my home, wrapped in burlap with other treasured playthings.

But it would be boring to dig for bones now. And we were sick of trying to sail paper boats in the standing pool above the drain pipe. It was choked with muck, too sluggish for real boat races.

Then a cat appeared in the rain and macabre gloom of the yard. We were suddenly alert as flies.

It was an East Side gutter cat, its head was gaunt, its bones jutted sharply like parts of a strange machine. It was sick. Its belly dragged the ground, it was sick with a new litter. It paused before a garbage can, sniffing out food.

We yelled. In slow agony, its eyes cast about, as if searching for a friend. The starved mother-cat suspected our whoops of joy. It leaped on a garbage can and waited. It did not hump its back, it was too weary to show anger or fear. It waited.

And we pursued it like fiends, pelting it with offal. It scrambled hysterically up the fence. We heard it drop on heavy feet into the next yard. There other bored children sat in the rain.

2

THERE is nothing in this incident that ought to be recorded. There were thousands of cats on the East Side; one of the commonplace joys of childhood was to torture cats, chase them, drop them from steep roofs to see whether cats had nine lives.

It was a world of violence and stone, there were too many cats, there were too many children.

The stink of cats filled the tenement halls. Cats fought around each garbage can in the East Side struggle for life. These cats were not the smug purring pets of the rich, but outcasts, criminals and fiends. They were hideous with scars and wounds, their fur was torn, they were smeared with unimaginable sores and filth, their eyes glared dangerously. They were so desperate they would sometimes fight a man. At

night they alarmed the tenement with their weird
cries like a congress of crazy witches. The obscene
heartbreak of their amours ruined our sleep, made us
cry and toss in cat nightmares. We tortured them,
they tortured us. It was poverty.

When you opened the door of your home there was
always a crazy cat or two trying to claw its way inside. They would lie for days outside the door, brood-
ing on the smell of cooking until they went insane.

Kittens died quietly in every corner, rheumy-eyed,
feeble and old before they had even begun to learn
to play.

Sometimes momma let you pity a kitten, give it a
saucer of milk which it lapped madly with its tiny
tongue.

But later you had to drive it out again into the
cruel street. There were too many kittens. The sorrow
of kittens was too gigantic for one child's pity.

I chased and persecuted cats with the other children; I never had much pity; but on this rainy afternoon I pitied the poor mother-cat.

I found myself thinking: Did God make cats?

3

I WAS oppressed with thoughts of God because my
parents had put me in a *Chaider*. I went to this Jewish
religious school every afternoon when the American
public school let out.

There is no hell fire in the orthodox Jewish religion. Children are not taught to harrow themselves searching for sin; nor to fear the hereafter. But they must memorize a long rigmarole of Hebrew prayers.

Reb Moisha was my teacher. This man was a walking, belching symbol of the decay of orthodox Judaism. What could such as he teach any one? He was ignorant as a rat. He was a foul smelling, emaciated beggar who had never read anything, or seen anything, who knew absolutely nothing but this sterile memory course in dead Hebrew which he whipped into the heads and backsides of little boys.

He dressed always in the same long black alpaca coat, green and disgusting with its pattern of grease, snuff, old food stains and something worse; for this religious teacher had nothing but contempt for the modern device of the handkerchief. He blew his nose on the floor, then wiped it on his horrible sleeve. Pickled herring and onions were his standard food. The sirocco blast of a thousand onions poured from his beard when he bent over the *Aleph-Beth* with you, his face close and hot to yours.

He was cruel as a jailer. He had a sadist's delight in pinching boys with his long pincer fingers; he was always whipping special offenders with his cat-o'-nine-tails; yet he maintained no real discipline in his hell-hole of Jewish piety.

I was appalled when my parents brought me there,

and after paying Reb Moisha his first weekly fee of fifty cents, left me with him.

In the ratty old loft, lit by a gas jet that cast a charnelhouse flare on the strange scene, I beheld thirty boys leaping and rioting like so many tigers pent in the one cage.

Some were spinning tops; others played tag, or wrestled; a group kneeled in a corner, staring at the ground as though a corpse lay there, and screaming passionately. They were shooting craps.

One of these boys saw me. He came over, and without a word, tore the picture of W. J. Bryan from my lapel. The boys gambled in buttons. He wanted my valuable button, so he took it.

At a long table, hacked by many knives, Reb Moisha sat with ten surly boys, the beginners' class. Soon I was howling with them. Over and over again we howled the ancient Hebrew prayers for thunder and lightning and bread and death; meaningless sounds to us. And Reb Moisha would pinch a boy, and scream above the bedlam, "Louder, little thieves! Louder!" He forced us to howl.

There was a smell like dead-dog from the broken toilet in the hall. A burlap curtain hung at one end of the hall to disguise the master's home, for he was the unlucky father of five children. His wife's harpy voice nagged them; we could smell onions frying; always onions for the master.

His face was white and sharp like a corpse's; it was framed in an inkblack beard; he wore a skullcap. His eyes glittered, and roved restlessly like an ogre's hungry for blood of little boys.

I hated this place. Once he tried to whip me, and instead of the usual submission, I ran home. My mother was angry.

"You must go back," she said. "Do you want to grow up into an ignorant *goy?*"

"But why do I have to learn all those Hebrew words? They don't mean anything, momma!"

"They mean a lot," said she severely. "Those are God's words, the way He wants us to pray to Him!"

"Who is God?" I asked. "Why must we pray to Him?"

"He is the one who made the world," said my mother solemnly. "We must obey Him."

"Did He make *everything?*"

"Yes, everything. God made everything in this world."

This impressed me. I returned to the *Chaider.* In the midst of the riot and screaming I would brood on my mother's God, on the strange man in the sky who must be addressed in Hebrew, that man who had created everything on earth.

4

MY mother was very pious. Her face darkened solemnly and mysteriously when she talked about her God. Every one argued about God. Mendel Bum, and Fyfka the Miser, and my Aunt Lena, and Jake Wolf, the saloonkeeper, and the fat janitor woman, and Mrs. Ashkenazi, of the umbrella store, and Mottke Blinder, and Harry the Pimp—all were interested in God. It was an important subject. When I discovered this, it became important for me, too.

I couldn't get the thought out of my head; God made everything. A child carries such thoughts about him unconsciously, the way he carries his body. They grow inside him. He sits quietly; no one knows why; he himself doesn't know. He is thinking. Then one day he will speak.

5

IN the livery stable on our street there was an old truck horse I loved. Every night he came home weary from work, but they did not unhitch him at once. He was made to wait for hours in the street by Vassa.

The horse was hungry. That's why he'd steal apples or bananas from the pushcarts if the peddler was napping. He was kicked and beaten for this, but it did not break him of his bad habit. They should have fed him sooner after a hard day's work. He was always neglected, and dirty, fly-bitten, gall-ridden. He was nicknamed the Ganuf—the old Thief on our street.

I stole sugar from home and gave it him. I stroked his damp nose, gray flanks, and gray tangled mane. He shook his head, and stared at me with his large gentle eyes. He never shook his head for the other boys; they marveled at my power over Ganuf.

He was a kind, good horse, and wise in many ways. For instance: Jim Bush abused him. Jim Bush was a fiery little Irish cripple who lived by doing odd jobs for the prostitute girls. Jim Bush was a tough guy only from the waist up. His blue fireman's shirt covered massive shoulders and arms. His face was red and leathery like a middle-aged cop's. But his legs were shriveled like a baby's.

He cracked dirty jokes with the girls, he was genial when sober. When he was drunk he wanted to fight every one. He would leap from his crutches at a man's throat and hang there like a bulldog, squeezing for death with his powerful hands, until beaten into unconsciousness. He always began his pugnacious debauches by abusing Ganuf the Horse.

He seemed to hate Ganuf. Why, I don't know. Maybe to show his power. Jim was the height of a boy of seven. He stood there, eyes bloodshot with liquor, mouth foaming, and shouted curses at the horse. Ganuf moved; Jim struck him over the nose with a crutch. Jim grabbed the bridle. "Back up!"

he yelled, then he sawed the bit on poor Ganuf's tongue. Then he clutched the horse's nostrils and tried to tear them off.

The poor horse was patient. He looked down from his great height at the screaming little cripple, and seemed to understand. He would have kicked any one else, but I think he knew Jim Bush was a cripple.

People always marveled at this scene. I used to feel sorry for my poor horse, and imagine there were tears in his eyes.

This horse dropped at work one summer day. They loosened his harness, and slopped buckets of water over him. He managed to stand up, but was weak. He dragged the truck back to the stable. Waiting there as usual to be unhitched for his supper, he fell gasping; he died on our street.

His body bloated like a balloon. He was left for a day until the wagon came to haul him to the boneyard.

When a horse lay dead in the street that way, he was seized upon to become another plaything in the queer and terrible treasury of East Side childhood.

Children gathered around Ganuf. They leaped on his swollen body, poked sticks in the vents. They pried open the eyelids, and speculated on those sad, glazed big eyes. They plucked hair from the tail with which to weave good-luck rings.

The fat blue and golden flies swarmed, too, around the body of my kind old friend. They buzzed and sang with furious joy as they attacked this tremendous meal sent them by the God of Flies.

I stood there helplessly. I wanted to cry for my poor old Ganuf. Had God made Ganuf? Then why had He let Ganuf die? And had God made flies?

The millions of East Side flies, that drove us crazy in summer, and sucked at our eyelids, while we slept, drowned in our glass of milk?

Why?

6

DID God make bedbugs? One steaming hot night I couldn't sleep for the bedbugs. They have a peculiar nauseating smell of their own; it is the smell of poverty. They crawl slowly and pompously, bloated with blood, and the touch and smell of these parasites wakens every nerve to disgust.

(Bedbugs are what people mean when they say: Poverty. There are enough pleasant superficial liars writing in America. I will write a truthful book of Poverty; I will mention bedbugs.)

It wasn't a lack of cleanliness in our home. My mother was as clean as any German housewife; she slaved, she worked herself to the bone keeping us fresh and neat. The bedbugs were a torment to her. She doused the beds with kerosene, changed the sheets, sprayed the mattresses in an endless frantic war with the bedbugs. What was the use; nothing could help; it was Poverty; it was the Tenement.

The bedbugs lived and bred in the rotten walls of the tenement, with the rats, fleas, roaches; the whole rotten structure needed to be torn down; a kerosene bottle would not help.

It had been a frightful week of summer heat. I was sick and feverish with heat, and pitched and tossed, while the cats sobbed in the yard. The bugs finally woke me. They were everywhere. I cannot tell the despair, loathing and rage of the child in the dark tenement room, as they crawled on me, and stank.

I cried softly. My mother woke and lit the gas. She renewed her futile battle with the bedbugs. The kerosene smell choked me. My mother tried to soothe me back to sleep. But my brain raced like a sewing machine.

"Momma," I asked, "why did God make bedbugs?"

She laughed at her little boy's quaint question. I was often jollied about it later, but who has answered this question? Did the God of Love create bedbugs, did He also put pain and poverty into the world? Why, a kind horse like my Ganuf would never have done such a thing.

CHAPTER 6

THE MISER AND THE BUM

1

WHEN I woke of a morning, I was never greatly surprised to find in my bed a new family of immigrants, in their foreign baggy underwear.

They looked pale and exhausted. They smelled of Ellis Island disinfectant, a stink that sickened me like castor oil.

Around the room was scattered their wealth, all their striped calico seabags, and monumental bundles of featherbeds, pots, pans, fine peasant linen, embroidered towels, and queer coats thick as blankets.

Every tenement home was a Plymouth Rock like ours. The hospitality was taken for granted until the new family rented its own flat. The immigrants would sit around our supper table, and ask endless questions about America. They would tell the bad news of the old country (the news was always bad). They would worry the first morning as to how to find work. They would be instructed that you must not blow out the gas (most of them had never seen it before). They would walk up and down our East Side street, peering at policemen and saloons in amazement at America.

They would make discoveries; they would chatter and be foolish.

After a few days they left us with thanks. But some stayed on and on, eating at our table. Don't think my mother liked this. We were too poor to be generous. She'd grumble about some one like Fyfka the Miser, grumble, curse, spit and mutter, but she'd never really ask him to move out. She didn't know how.

2

IMAGINE the kind of man this Fyfka the Miser was. We did not even know him when he came from Ellis Island. He said he was the friend of the cousin of a boyhood friend of my father's. He had our address and the name of this distant, mythical, and totally unknown friend of the cousin of a friend in Roumania. Nothing more; and we didn't like him from the start; but for seven months he ate and slept at our home— for nothing.

He was squat, with a glum black muzzle, and nostrils like a camel. A thatch of black uncombed hair fell down his forehead, over small eyes, too bright and too morbid, like a baboon's. One arm was twisted, and he never smiled, he never said a pleasant word, he was always scratching himself, he never cleaned his nose.

Fyfka got a job in a pants factory a week after he arrived; good pay for an immigrant, eight dollars a

week. He worked from six A.M. to seven at night.
Every morning he bought two rolls for a penny. One
roll and a glass of water was his breakfast. For lunch
he ate the other roll, and a three-cent slice of herring.

Every night, time exactly right, just as we were
finishing supper, he came home. He sat himself
gloomily in the same chair in the corner of the room,
and watched as we ate. He didn't say a word, just sat
and watched. It got on your nerves; your food choked
you as you felt that dumb, gloomy, animal face in the
room.

When the tension became too great, and all conversation had been dampened by the silent stranger,
my father would spring from the table.

"*Nu*, Fyfka," he would say bitterly, as if defeated
in a contest, "draw up and eat something, for God's
sake. There's still some soupmeat left."

So Fyfka drew up his chair, and would eat, gobble
and grab, with a slinky look at us out of the corner of
his eye, like a dog.

All this took place every night in the same way,
like a well-rehearsed farce at a theater. It's a wonder
neither Fyfka nor my parents sickened of the farce.
My mother gently suggested to him once that he move,
and he began to whine and cry and say he had no
money. My father (in private) threatened to take
Fyfka by the collar and throw him out some day, but
he never did.

Fyfka paid us no rent; he never changed his shirt or the clothes he had worn in the steerage; he went to no picnics, parks or theaters; he didn't smoke, or drink, or eat candy; he needed nothing.

Thus out of eight dollars a week he managed to save some two hundred dollars in the months he sponged on us. He had heard of Rothschild. He wanted to go into business in America. Poverty makes some people insane.

3

This thing, this Fyfka the Miser, this yellow somnambulist, this nightmare bred of poverty; this maggot-yellow dark ape with twisted arm and bright, peering, melancholy eyes; human garbage can of horror; fevered Rothschild in a filthy shirt; madman in an old derby hat:

This perfection had a flaw; this monster needed women.

This Caliban was tortured, behind his low puckered forehead, by a horrible conflict between body and mind.

Our East Side was then administered by Tammany Hall as a red light district. My childhood street, as I have said, was a marketplace of loud, painted women in kimonos, transacting the oldest business in the world. Stores, tenement flats, furnished rooms and even the alleys waited for this Caliban's body's peace.

But it would cost money. This miser watched the

busy women night after night until he could endure
it no longer. He came to know some of them, clutched
at them, stole contacts, groveled before them to be
kind. He came to be the joke of the neighborhood—
the madman who wanted a woman, but was too stingy
to pay the regular price of fifty cents.

"Yah, yah!" Mendel Bum jeered him at our supper
table. "Fyfka tried to touch that fat Sarah in the
hallway to-night, and she slapped him, and screamed.
The pimps will yet stab you for this, Fyfka!"

"It's a lie, I never touched her!" the monster
shouted. "I don't care for women. All they want is
your money."

"Don't talk of such things before the children,"
said my mother.

"*Nu*, give the girls money, then!" said Mendel
laughing, as he winked at my father. "That's what
money is for, Fyfka; not to be hidden in a corner,
for the rats to eat. Money was made for fun; look at
me, how fat and healthy I am, because I spend my
money!"

Fyfka glared at him. Hate for the jovial Mendel
made the big cords swell in his neck; the miser trembled with hate.

"It's a lie; I've got no money. I don't save money;
why do you spread such lies about me? You're a liar!
and a bum! a bum!"

"Sure, I'm a bum," said Mendel cheerfully, "so

every one likes me, Fyfka. But you're a miser, and you every one hates. Yah!"

"Gerarahere, mind your own business!"

Fyfka snarled like an ape, every one laughed at his grotesque rage, he got up from the table.

"Don't talk about such things before the children," said my mother.

But everything was talked before us, we heard everything, and knew the strange world.

4

MENDEL had been a sailor; an anchor was tattooed on his strong left arm. Tattooing is forbidden to Jews; the body must be returned to God as He created it. Mendel also freely ate pork and ham, and did other things forbidden to Jews. One winter he capped all these blasphemies by the supreme sin. He went the rounds of the Bowery missions, and permitted each in turn to baptize him. For this he received money, sacks of potatoes, suits of clothes, various odd jobs, and a chance to learn the cornet.

My mother was horrified when she discovered how Mendel had earned the groceries he brought her.

"Take them at once out of my house," she said, "those Christian potatoes!"

"Aren't all potatoes good when you're hungry?" asked Mendel, slyly.

"No. To sell your Jewish soul for a sack of pota-

toes—to be baptized—it's a sin, Mendel! Your
momma in Hungary would die if she knew about it."

"How will she know about it, will I tell her?"
Mendel protested. "And who says I'm baptized? No,
momma, you're wrong; I wouldn't give up being a
Jew for anything. This is just a way of making a
living; I am out of work, so why should I starve?
Those Christians, a black year on them, are so crazy
to have Jews baptized they even pay for it. So what
do I do—I fool them. I let them sprinkle their water
on me—and all the time, under my breath, I am
cursing them, I am saying, to hell with your idol! to
hell with your holy water! When they are through, I
take my potatoes and go—but I am the same Mendel
still, a Jew among Jews!"

My mother, like every one else, was bewildered by
the flow of Mendel's glib charlatan logic.

"And the baptism doesn't mean anything, you're
still a Jew, Mendel?"

"Of course, I'm a Jew, a firm Jew, a good Jew,
and these are my potatoes now—they're Jewish
potatoes. But I won't be baptized again, I promise it,"
he said.

Mendel lived with us about twice a year, when his
bum's luck failed him elsewhere. He did everything—
peddled needle threaders, acted in a burlesque show,
enlisted in the Spanish-American War only to desert
before the fighting began. He had been with cowboys

and Indians out west, a miner, a barber in Rio de
Janeiro, a prisoner in Chattanooga, Tennessee, a
lemonade vendor with a circus, a Turk at Coney
Island, runner for a gambling house, a thousand other
things.

Every one liked him, even my mother. He was
husky, cheerful, with red hair, blue eyes, and a
humorous face. He brought gales of bold life into the
stale bedrooms of the East Side. It was amusing to
Jews that Mendel could fool Americans with his
tricks. It was flattering to Jews to know that he often
passed himself off as a real American, yet talked
Yiddish and was loyal to his race.

CHAPTER 7

THE GOLDEN BEAR

1

MY father, a house painter, was a tall lively man with Slavic cheek bones and a red mustache. His large green eyes stared at the world like a child's. He was full of temperament, and my mother had to manage him constantly.

With female realism she tried to beat the foolish male dreams out of his head. But she never succeeded in converting my father into a sober family person. Alas, he was a man of quicksilver!

Jews are as individualized as are Chinese or Anglo-Saxons. There are no racial types. My father, for instance, was like a certain kind of Irishman more than the stenciled stage Jew.

He was born near Yassy, Roumania. He had wandered along the Danube and through the Balkans. He had lived in the slums of Constantinople, and had been with a band of young Jews who smuggled tobacco from Turkey into Roumania.

He often told us stories of his old-world youth, and we children loved to hear them.

My father was an unusual story-teller. Had he received an education, he might have become a fine

writer. I envied him then, and I envy him yet, his
streak of naïve genius.

For years he soothed my little sister and me to
sleep with his delightfully fantastic tales. They were
inexhaustible; each night there was a new one, told
in the darkness against the evening throb of the
tenement.

Some of the stories haunted me, they colored all
my childhood. Years later I read them with amazement in a book. They were nothing more or less than
the Arabian Nights.

But my father had not learned them out of a book.
He had heard them from the lips of professional
story-tellers in Oriental market-places, or from Turkish and Roumanian peasants.

2

MY father was passionately social. Like many Jews,
he loved to eat, sleep, laugh and weep in the midst of
a crowd. If he ever found himself alone, he became
moody and imagined he was sick. Every night in our
house there was a convention of my father's friends,
housepainters, peddlers, clothing workers and other
Jews struggling in the promised land.

Poker and pinochle for penny stakes were fought
over bitterly. Sometimes they drank tea and philosophized. Sometimes they went to wine cellars and drank
wine.

Very often, my father told stories. Some of his stories took weeks to tell, five or six hours each night. No one thought it unusual that my father should know hundreds of stories. He himself thought it as natural as breathing. These Jews came from the world of peasant Europe, where art is inherited with one's father's farm, and is a simple fact of life.

Strange tableau! my father sprawled on the couch smoking his pipe, the gas jet dimmed to a point to save gas, and a dozen sweatshop workers breathing and stirring in the darkness as they listened to my father narrate the thousand-year-old fables of the Orient.

His voice was heard in the dark. It changed with the moods of the story. Now it was fierce with the basso rumblings of the Executioner of Constantinople. Then it grew tender as a Snow-Maiden's, or as the voice of the love-racked young Mountain Prince. Then it was an old witch's shrill voice, or a drunken Turkish giant's. My father had the makings of an actor.

My sister and I never tired of his stories. The grown-up pants pressers and housepainters seemed as fascinated. Even my realistic mother sat down to listen. Neighbors dropped in, graybeard grandfathers with snuff boxes; tired mommas in aprons; men and women who sat hypnotized like children.

They held long debates after each story. Like earnest children, they discussed villains, and magic mountains, and wishing lamps as if this mythology were as real as the sweatshops and garbage cans.

3

MY father, too, must have believed some of his own stories. There was one story, The Golden Bear, that he told oftener and with more skill than the rest.

I can see, in the newsreel of memory, the scene on our roof when I first heard this story.

Many summer nights we climbed to the roof. Cans of beer and salami sandwiches were brought along, and my father told stories while we ate and drank.

Moon and stars shone from the black sky that covered New York. My father's face gleamed mysteriously in the starlight. He smoked a cigar. Behind him stood a cardboard jumble of tenement chimneys and skyscrapers.

He spoke in the low, sure, magnetic voice of a master. He knew his power, and gained a strange dignity when he was telling a story. On the roof, aided by moon and stars, he became doubly magical.

"Once upon a time," he began quietly and gravely, "there lived a hunter in Brescu. It is a Roumanian village near the one from which I come. It is on the river Ved. One cold morning this hunter went out to shoot a bear. The wind howled, the hunter fought through snow up to his waist. The frost bit into his rags like a dog's tooth. This hunter hated the cold.

It reminded him of his poverty. His father was a peasant, but his mother had been a Turkish girl. Often she said to the hunter when he was a child:

"'My son, when you grow up you must go to Turkey. There, in the south, it is warm. The roses bloom in December, and the birds sing. No one is poor there, every one has enough. Promise me you will escape there, my son. I want to see you happy.'

"The hunter promised. He had always dreamed of going there. But he married, and raised a family, and found himself a man in a trap. How could he take his family to Turkey? He had no money. He was so poor he did not even own a piece of land.

"That is why, on this bitter cold morning, he was angry when he set off to hunt. As he walked, freezing and groaning, he dreamed of the south. Suddenly in the woods near his village, he saw marks of a huge bear. He followed the footprints through the snow until he came to a cave. There, his gun pointed before him, he entered.

"What he found was three little cubs at play. He was about to kill them, and hide until the mother came, when she, too, entered. She was the largest and most beautiful bear he had ever seen. Her fur was the color of golden money.

"The hunter was frightened. He lifted his gun to shoot her. Suddenly this Golden Bear spoke to him in Roumanian.

"Clasping her paws in prayer, the bear said in a mother's sorrowful voice:

" 'Dear, good hunter,' she said, 'I know you are poor, and need to kill us in order to provide food for your own family. But spare my little ones,' she said. 'I will pay anything you ask,' she said. 'I know magic secrets known only to Golden Bears, and will help you,' she said.

" 'Can you help me take my family to Turkey, and find us land there?' the hunter asked.

" 'Yes,' said the Golden Bear, 'if you spare my cubs. It will be a difficult journey, because there are witches, magicians, and angry tyrants on that road. But I promise to take you to Turkey. And I promise you will never need money all your life.'

" 'Agreed,' said the hunter."

4

THIS story of the Golden Bear took three weeks to tell; the road to Turkey was crowded with strange happenings. The story was the eternal fable of the man to whom the good things of life come by magic. All poor men believe in such magic, and dream of the day when they will stumble on it. My father was one of the many.

So he told this story with great feeling, and I remember hearing it on the tenement roof, under the night sky of New York. Hung like tall ships with red and white lamps, the skyscrapers stood up against the moon. Tropical breezes blew in from the ocean. From the street, the East Side traffic throbbed like a great drum.

5

THE Jews have been known as "the people of the book." Shut for twenty centuries from the life of deeds, the broken Jewish nation learned to revere its writers and men of thought.

My father and his friends, uneducated manual workers, shared a strong, reverent passion for the theater.

Some of them would go to a favorite play, ten and twenty times. Each had his worshiped actor. Each felt himself a subtle dramatic critic.

My father, with his memory for fiction, had an advantage over the others. He could repeat entire scenes of the plays he had seen, and act them out.

His favorite drama was "The Robbers," by Schiller. He boasted that he had seen this play thirty-four times, in Yiddish, German, Russian and Roumanian. He could recite it almost from beginning to end.

Others of his favorite plays were Gorky's "Night's Lodging," Hauptmann's "The Weavers," Tolstoy's "Kreutzer Sonata," Goldfaden's lovely and naïve music-drama, "The Witch," and "Hamlet."

These plays, and others like them, were popular

on the Yiddish boards years ago. The garment
workers lived with Shakespeare. To-day the Yiddish
stage is Americanized. It produces imitations of
Broadway musical comedy.

In the steerage on the way to America, my father
evolved the curious idea that Schiller's play, "The
Robbers," was unknown in America, and that he
would introduce it here.

Through a storm lasting eleven days, my father
wrote out the play in Yiddish, with a lead pencil on
letter sheets.

As soon as he established himself in New York, he
began plaguing the well-known Yiddish actor,
Mogelescu, for an interview. Granted this, my father
tried to read the play to the tragedian.

Mogelescu laughed. "The play is already in my
repertoire," he said. "Did you think such a great play
could remain unknown even in America?"

My father retired in gloomy confusion. During the
rest of his life he repeated this anecdote, and would
add: "Always I have been too late."

I think my father got the feeling at times that he
himself was the author of "The Robbers," and that
Mogelescu had cheated him of his rights.

CHAPTER 8

THE PROMISED BRIDE

1

MY sister Esther lay in one bed, I was in the other. The bedroom was dark, except for a tiny tip of gaslight.

It was twelve at night. Children kept the same hours as grownups on the East Side.

My eyelids were heavy with sleep. My sister was drowsy, too. Our father's story was like a waking dream. As he talked in his hypnotic voice, the story entered us, and became something that was happening to us in a dream.

My father sat on a chair between the two beds, smoking his pipe. Now and then he stroked Esther's face or mine.

Sounds floated from the airshaft. Mrs. Fingerman's parrot was growling and chuckling in a pirate's voice. A clothesline squeaked. A woman hung out her washing. A baby cried. The tank on the roof was always overflowing. Drowsy water slid down the airshaft walls. Plates rattled, a sewing machine hummed.

Under these sounds, we felt the swell of the East Side traffic, like an ocean in moonlight, while our father told us the story of his life.

2

"I WAS always in trouble in Roumania," said my father. "There was a devil in me, that would not let me rest.

"I was always fighting and drinking, and my father did not know what to do with me. I had hot blood, and did things for which I am now ashamed.

"I will not tell about the time my father sent me to travel from village to village. I was to buy pottery and grain from the peasants for his business.

"He gave me two hundred dollars. I spent it on foolishness in a week. I was so ashamed of myself I did not return home for a year.

"Then I came back in rags. I was forgiven. A year later, I ran away to Constantinople. I was caught at the tobacco smuggling and put in a prison on the frontier. I wrote a letter to my father, and he came and bribed the Mayor of the village, and took me out.

"But I will not tell you about all that. *Nu*, I was just a young fool!

3

"THE worst thing I did was to refuse to marry the bride pledged to me before I was born. Her name was Miriam Glotzer.

"In the old country it is a disgrace to have only female children. Every orthodox Jew prays to have male descendants, too, so that these can say *Kaddish* for him when he is dead, and keep his name alive in the world.

"It is also bad to have nothing but male children, and no girls. The Talmud instructs us that there must be both male and female in a family.

"My mother, may she rest in peace, had borne four girls, and she feared she would go through life without a male child. She decided to visit a famous Rabbi and ask for his help.

"Moisha Glotzer's wife, a neighbor, went with her. This woman wanted to beg the Rabbi to help her bear a female child. Her family consisted of only boys.

"The Rabbi lived in a village forty miles away. He was a famous Rabbi, and proved worthy of his reputation. He performed a miracle for my mother and her neighbor.

"To my mother the Rabbi said without hesitation: 'God will help you. Go home, be patient, in a year you will bear a male child, a *ben zucher*.

" 'When he is born, tell your husband to bring me a living fish, and I will give you a name for the child.'

"To Moisha Glotzer's wife the Rabbi said, stroking his beard thoughtfully: 'May God help you have a girl. Nothing is certain with God.'

"My mother was full of joy. The other woman was not so pleased, yet was hopeful. On the journey home she said to my mother: 'It is certain you will have a boy. I feel as sure that I will have a girl.

Our husbands have the same standing in the community. Let us show our trust in God by pledging our unborn children in marriage.'

"My mother agreed. At the next village where the stagecoach stopped they invited a number of Jews to witness the pledging, and to eat honey cake and drink brandy. It is an old Jewish custom, this betrothal of children before birth. Here in America it has been forgotten, thank God.

"*Nu*, within a year, exactly as the Rabbi had promised, my mother bore a son: myself, and Mrs. Glotzer was granted a daughter.

"This miracle made the Rabbi even more famous. Every Jew in trouble and every woman wanting a child came to him from the most distant places in Roumania and Galicia when this miracle was reported.

"After my birth, my father traveled to the Rabbi to bring him a living fish as he had commanded, and to pay him money, and to get from him my name.

"The Rabbi accepted the fish and money, and gave me a name. Then he said to my father: 'That the child may live to manhood and wealth, follow these instructions of mine. When you come to your home, before you enter, dig some earth from under your doorsill. Then from the ceiling on your right hand as you go in, carefully remove a spider's web. Then go to the market-place, and the first beggar you see, be

he Jew or Gentile, ask him for a penny and a crust
of bread. Then take all these things, tie them into a
red piece of cloth, and hang it around the child's
throat. This will be his charm through life against
sickness, accident and witchcraft.'

"Another instruction: 'Dress the child in nothing
but white linen, until the day when he makes a
protest.'

"All this was done. And it brought me some of the
greatest grief my life has known.

4

"First, because of the commandment of the white
linen. I was marked among my playmates because I
was dressed so strangely in nothing but white. The
boys teased me, sometimes calling me the Priest, and
at other times, the Little Corpse.

"One day, when I was four years old, I came home
crying after having been teased. I said to my mother:
'Momma, go to the marketplace and buy me some
blue clothing. I won't dress in white any longer.'

"The change was made immediately. My parents
were joyful. All had come about as the Rabbi had
prophesied; he was surely a miracle-worker. From
then on I was not forced to wear white.

5

"BUT not so easily ended the sorrow caused by my promised bride. If my playmates had teased me when I dressed in white, they more than tortured me when they learned the story of my betrothal. For years, as I grew up, my only nickname among them was the *Chusen*—the Little Bridegroom.

"What fun they had with the name. How many fights I went through because of my misfortune. It made me hate Miriam, my promised bride.

"She was a quiet little girl, with black hair and eyes, and of a kind nature. But I pulled her hair and slapped her face whenever we met.

" 'Go away, I hate you,' I would say. Tears flowed from her eyes and she would go away.

"Once she complained to my mother. 'Auntie,' she said, 'why does Herman beat me? I like him so much and yet he beats me.'

"I spoke up: 'I beat her because it is her fault every one calls me the Little Bridegroom. I refuse to marry her.'

"Her father was a butcher. He sold black untaxed whisky to the peasants, and lent out money. He cheated the peasants, and was a well-to-do man. He used to come to our home, and pat my head.

" '*Nu*, how is my little *mashkin*, my pledged one?' he said.

"He acted toward me as if I were his property, his son. It made me very angry even as a child. It hung over me like a cloud.

"He used to inspect me, and feel my legs and shoulders and neck, in the same suspicious way he, the butcher, bought cattle at the peasant fairs.

"And he would ask me Talmud questions, to see if I were a good student. Thus it continued for years. I hated it all, but was too afraid to speak out.

"One spring day in my sixteenth year, this man arrived in his best Sabbath suit at my home.

" 'The time has come,' he said to my father. 'Let us draw up the contract for the engagement of our children.'

"My father agreed. The date was settled for the following week. Suddenly I was in despair. I had a good friend, a boy named Simon, who was very clever. 'Simon,' I said, 'I do not want to be engaged. I do not want to marry this girl. What shall I do?'

" 'Nothing,' he answered. 'There is nothing you can do. You should have spoken sooner; now it is too late.'

6

"My father took me to the tailor and had made a handsome velvet *yamalka* and velvet hat. Then he took me to the shoemaker, and had made fine bast boots for me.

"Presents were exchanged between the two families. Miriam's father sent me a fur coat, and a wonderful parchment Talmud, and a gold watch. My father sent to Miriam a white silk bridal dress, a ring, and a gold chain set with pearls that had belonged to my great-grandmother and was precious.

"The following week, in a carriage drawn by the best team of horses in the village, we set off for the home of my promised bride.

"My heart burned like a fire. Every one laughed and drank brandy on the way, but I wanted to cry. Too late, too late, I should have protested against this marriage years ago!

7

"MIRIAM's home was crowded with friends and relatives. They were eating, and drinking and dancing. Wine, brandy, stuffed geese, cakes and preserves of all kinds, nuts, fruits, everything was there in abundance.

"Two old Jewish fiddlers and a clarinet made jolly music. People gave me wine to drink, and I drank it. But it failed to make me happy. I was thinking of what to do.

"Miriam came over and talked to me in her quiet way. She was a lovely girl. She was a good girl, a modest girl. I had a queer feeling as I looked at her. I might have fallen in love with her, had not I been forced to marry her. That is what I felt.

" 'Herman, why don't you ever talk to me?' she asked quietly. 'For ten years you have never talked to me.'

" 'There is nothing to talk about,' I said. 'Everything is settled.'

" 'But you are a good Talmud student,' she said. 'Let us talk about the Talmud.'

" 'No,' I said. 'I am a bad Talmud student.'

" 'You go to the theaters, and know many plays,' she said. 'Let us discuss plays and poetry, Herman.'

" 'No,' I said, cruelly, 'I do not discuss such things with women. The birds of the air despise a man who is weak with women.'

"I was saying this only to hurt her, yet it hurt me, too.

8

"IN the next room sat my father and Miriam's father and various relatives and a Rabbi. They were settling the contract for our marriage.

"At last they called me in. I turned pale when the message came, and drank off a glass of strong plum brandy. Suddenly I made up my mind not to marry.

"My knees shook when I came into that room where they sat with the contract spread on a table.

"My heart trembled. I did not know how to begin.

"My father said, 'Herman, everything has been settled. Sign the contract.'

"I said, looking him in the eye, 'Father, no, I cannot.'

"My father turned pale with surprise.

" 'What,' he said, 'you wish to disgrace me, you *goy*, you Christian?'

" 'Father,' I said, 'this is a good girl, a beautiful girl, but I refuse to marry her.'

" 'Why?' my father thundered.

" 'I don't know,' I said.

"My father slapped my face. I was a fighter then, and could have picked him up and broken him if he were not my father.

"But I stiffened my back, and looked at him proudly.

" 'Father, I am not a child any longer. For this I am going to leave you. I am going to America to make my fortune.'

" 'You will starve in the gutters there!' said my father. 'You will eat with the pigs. Go, you have blackened my name among the Jews of Roumania. You have broken the word your mother gave to Miriam's mother before you were born. Go, infidel, and eat the bread of sorrow and shame in America. I am no longer your father.'

"I left the engagement party. My action made a horrible scandal in our village, and Miriam grew sick. My father grew sick and died a year later. And every one felt it was because of my pride and folly.

"When I left for America every one repeated my father's words: he will eat the bread of sorrow and shame in America. He will never make his fortune."

~~~~~~

CHAPTER 9

SAM KRAVITZ, THAT THIEF

1

"WHY did I choose to come to America?" asked my father of himself gravely, as he twisted and untwisted his mustache in the darkness. "I will tell you why: it was because of envy of my dirty thief of a cousin, that Sam Kravitz, may his nose be eaten by the pox.

"All this time, while I was disgracing my family, Sam had gone to America, and was making his fortune. Letters came from him, and were read throughout our village. Sam, in two short years, already owned his own factory for making suspenders. He sent us his picture. It was marveled at by every one. Our Sam no longer wore a fur cap, a long Jewish coat and peasant boots. No. He wore a fine gentleman's suit, a white collar like a doctor, store shoes and a beautiful round fun-hat called a derby.

"He suddenly looked so fat and rich, this beggarly cobbler's son! I tell you, my liver burned with envy when I heard my father and mother praise my cousin Sam. I knew I was better than him in every way, and it hurt me. I said to my father, 'Give me money. Let me go at once to America to redeem myself. I will

make more money than Sam, I am smarter than he is.
You will see!'

"My mother did not want me to go. But my father
was weary of my many misfortunes, and he gave me
the money for the trip. So I came to America. It was
the greatest mistake in my life.

"One should not do things through envy. There is
a story in the Talmud that illustrates this. Once there
was a man who owned a beautiful little dog and a big
ugly jackass. Every night while eating his supper the
man would take the dog on his lap and feed it and
stroke its head affectionately. The dog would kiss him
and lick his face. The jackass watched this for a time,
and became envious.

"So one night at supper he entered the house and
sat himself on the man's lap, too. He licked the man's
face with his rough tongue, and embraced him affectionately with his legs.

"But the man did not stroke the jackass's head in
return, or feed him choice food. No, the man was very
angry. He took a stick and beat the surprised jackass
and chased him out of the house. The moral of this
is, do not envy other people's good luck.

2

"I am not discouraged, children. I will make a great
deal of money some day. I am a serious married man
now and no greenhorn. But then I was still a foolish

boy, and though I left Roumania with great plans in my head, in my heart a foolish voice was saying: 'America is a land of fun.'

"How full I was of all the *Baba* stories that were told in my village about America! In America, we believed, people dug under the streets and found gold anywhere. In America, the poorest ragpicker lived better than a Roumanian millionaire. In America, people did little work, but had fun all day.

"I had seen two pictures of America. They were shown in the window of a store that sold Singer Sewing Machines in our village. One picture had in it the tallest building I had ever seen. It was called a skyscraper. At the bottom of it walked the proud Americans. The men wore derby hats and had fine mustaches and gold watch chains. The women wore silks and satins, and had proud faces like queens. Not a single poor man or woman was there; every one was rich.

"The other picture was of Niagara Falls. You have seen the picture on postcards; with Indians and cowboys on horses, who look at a rainbow shining over the water.

"I tell you, I wanted to get to America as fast as I could, so that I might look at the skyscrapers and at the Niagara Falls rainbow, and wear a derby hat.

"In my family were about seventy-five relatives. All came to see me leave Roumania. There was much crying. But I was happy, because I thought I was going to a land of fun.

"The last thing my mother did, was to give me my cousin's address in New York, and say: 'Go to Sam. He will help you in the strange land.'

"But I made up my mind I would die first rather than ask Sam for help.

3

"WELL, for eleven days our boat rocked on the ocean. I was sick, but I wrote out a play called 'The Robbers' of Schiller and dreamed of America.

"They gave us dry herring and potatoes to eat. The food was like dung and the boat stank like a big water closet. But I was happy.

"I joked all the way. One night all of us young immigrants held a singing party. One young Roumanian had an accordion. We became good friends, because both of us were the happiest people on the boat.

"He was coming to a rich uncle, a cigarmaker who owned a big business, he said. When he learned I had no relatives in America, he asked me to live at his uncle's with him. I agreed, because I liked this boy.

"*Nu*, how shall I tell how glad we were when after eleven days on the empty ocean we saw the buildings of New York?

"It looked so nice and happy, this city standing on end like a child's toys and blocks. It looked like a land of fun, a game waiting for me to play.

"And in Ellis Island, where they kept us overnight, I slept on a spring bed that had no mattress, pillow or blankets. I was such a greenhorn that I had never seen a spring before. I thought it was wonderful, and bounced up and down on it for fun.

"Some one there taught me my first American words. All night my friend Yossel and I bounced up and down on the springs and repeated the new funny words to each other.

"Potato! he would yell at me. Tomato! I would answer, and laugh. Match! he would say. All right! I would answer. Match! all right! go to hell! potato! until every one was angry at us, the way we kept them awake with our laughing and yelling.

"In the morning his uncle came for us and took us home in a horsecar.

"I tell you my eyes were busy on that ride through the streets. I was looking for the American fun.

4

"*Nu*, I will not mention how bad I felt when I saw the cigarmaker uncle's home. It was just a big dirty dark room in the back of the cigar store where he made and sold cigars. He, his wife and four children lived in that one room.

"He was not glad to have me there, but he spread newspapers on the floor, and Yossel and I slept on them.

"What does it matter, I thought, this is not America. To-morrow morning I will go out in the streets, and see the real American fun.

5

"The next morning Yossel and I took a long walk. That we might not be lost, we fixed in our minds the big gold tooth of a dentist that hung near the cigar shop.

"We walked and walked. I will not tell you what we saw, because you see it every day. We saw the East Side. To me it was a strange sight. I could not help wondering, where are all the people running? What is happening? And why are they so serious? When does the fun start?

"We came to Allen Street, under the elevated. To show you what a greenhorn I was, I fell in love with the elevated train. I had never seen anything like it in Roumania.

"I was such a greenhorn I believed the elevated train traveled all over America, to Niagara Falls and other places. We rode up and down on it all day. I paid the fare.

"I had some money left. I also bought two fine derby hats from a pushcart; one for Yossel, and one

for me. They were a little big, but how proud we felt
in these American fun-hats.

"No one wears such hats in Roumania. Both of us
had pictures taken in the American fun-hats to send
to our parents.

6

"THIS foolishness went on for two weeks. Then all my
money was gone. So the cigarmaker told me I should
find a job and move out from his home. So I found
a job for seven dollars a month in a grocery store. I
lived over the store, I rose at five o'clock, and went to
bed at twelve in the night. My feet became large and
red with standing all day. The grocerman, may the
worms find him, gave me nothing to eat but dry bread,
old cheese, pickles and other stale groceries. I soon became sick and left that job.

"For a week I sat in Hester Park without a bite of
food. And I looked around me, but was not unhappy.
Because I tell you, I was such a greenhorn, that I still
thought fun would start and I was waiting for it.

"One night, after sleeping on the bench, I was very
hungry in the morning and decided to look up my
rich cousin, Sam Kravitz. I hated to do this, but was
weak with fasting. So I came into my cousin's shop.
To hide my shame I laughed out loud.

" 'Look, Sam, I am here,' I laughed. 'I have just
come off the boat, and am ready to make my fortune.'

"So my cousin Sam gave me a job in his factory. He paid me twenty-five cents a day.

"He had three other men working for him. He worked himself. He looked sick and sharp and poor and not at all like the picture of him in the fun-hat he had sent to Roumania.

7

"*Nu*, so your father worked. I got over my greenhorn idea that there was nothing but fun in America. I learned to work like every one else. I grew thin as my cousin.

"Soon I came to understand it was not a land of fun. It was a Land of Hurry-Up. There was no gold to be dug in the streets here. Derbies were not fun-hats for holidays. They were work-hats. *Nu*, so I worked! With my hands, my liver and sides! I worked!

8

"MY cousin Sam had fallen into a good trade. With his machines he manufactured the cotton ends of suspenders. These ends are made of cotton, and are very important to a suspender. It is these ends that fasten to the buttons, and hold up the pants. This is important to the pants, as you know.

"Yes, it was a good trade, and a necessary one. There was much money to be made, I saw that at once.

"But my cousin Sam was not a good business man.

He had no head for figures and his face was like vinegar. None of his customers liked him.

"Gradually, he let me go out and find business for him. I was very good for this. Most of the big suspender shops were owned by Roumanians who had known my father. They greeted me like a relative. I drank wine with them, and passed jokes. So they gave me their orders for suspender ends.

"So one day, seeing how I built up the business, Sam said: 'You shall be my partner. We are making a great deal of money. Leave the machine, Herman. I will take care of the inside shop work. You go out every day, and joke with our customers and bring in the orders.'

"So I was partners with my cousin Sam. So I was very happy. I earned as much as thirty dollars a week; I was at last a success.

"So a matchmaker came, and said I ought to marry. So he brought me to your momma and I saw at once that she was a kind and hard-working woman. So I decided to marry her and have children.

"So this was done.

9

"IT was then I made the greatest mistake of my life.

"Always I had wanted to see that big water with the rainbow and Indians called Niagara Falls.

"So I took your momma there when we married.

I spent a month's wages on the trip. I showed America to your momma. We enjoyed ourselves.

"In a week we came back. I went to the shop the next morning to work again. I could not find the shop. It had vanished. I could not find Sam. He had stolen the shop.

"I searched and searched for Sam and the shop. My heart was swollen like a sponge with hate. I was ready to kill my cousin Sam.

"So one day I found him and the shop. I shouted at him, 'Thief, what have you done?' He laughed. He showed me a paper from a lawyer proving that the shop was his. All my work had been for nothing. It had only made Sam rich.

"What could I do? So in my hate I hit him with my fist, and made his nose bleed. He ran into the street yelling for a policeman. I ran after him with a stick, and beat him some more. But what good could it do? The shop was really his, and I was left a pauper.

10

"So now I work as a house painter. I work for another man, I am not my own master now. I am a man in a trap.

"But I am not defeated. I am a man with a strong will. I will yet have another shop. All I need is three hundred dollars; and I will find this three hundred dollars somehow.

"Yes! yes! I will show my cousin yet! I will show the world how I can run a suspender ends shop!

"I will have no partners this time. I will work alone. I will show your mother how a man makes his fortune in America! Look at Nathan Straus! Look at Otto Kahn! They peddled shoe laces when they first came here! I have had a better start, and should go farther than they!

"I am certain to be rich! I will make a school teacher out of you, Esther! You will dress in a fine waist and a pompadour and be a teacher. Isn't that wonderful, Esther?"

"Yes, poppa."

"And you, Mikey, will be a doctor! You will be what I would have been had I kissed a priest's hand. It is a great thing to be a doctor. It is better to have wisdom than to have money. I will earn the money, Mikey, and make you a doctor! How do you like that? Will you do it?"

"Yes, poppa," I said sleepily.

CHAPTER 10

×××××××××××××××××××××××××××××××××××××××

A HOUSE PAINTER'S TEARS

1

IT was summer. My father worked on a scaffold in the sun. One day he grew dizzy with the painter's disease—lead poisoning.

Paint is made with white lead. When a house painter mixes oil and turpentine with the dry pigment, its lead is released in fumes which the man must breathe. Or this free lead also enters through the skin. It eats up the painter's stomach and nerves, and poisons his bones.

My father suffered from painter's nausea. One summer night he came home after his accustomed hour. His pale face under its tattoo of green and red paint was twisted grotesquely, like a Chinese dancer's mask. He stripped off his overalls in the kitchen and sank into a chair.

"Quick! give me the bucket, Katie!" he groaned to my mother. She brought it, and he vomited. She held his head, and patted his shoulder. "I have been sick all afternoon," he groaned.

"*Nu, nu,*" said my mother gently, "it will pass, Herman."

His body shook with spasms of violent retching,

and he cried. My mother never cried, but my father wept easily.

"Why must I work at this accursed trade?" my father wept, hiccoughing, "to fall off a scaffold some day, maybe, and break my legs, and then come at the lunch hour every day to other painters, to beg them for a little money? Every day there comes one of them, the sick painters."

"*Nu, nu*, Herman," my mother soothed him, "it will not happen to you."

"It *will* happen," my father wept. "I am always the unfortunate one. And if that doesn't happen, I will die of this paint sickness, I am sure of it. And once I owned a suspender shop of my own! Once I worked for myself and laughed and lived! But now I must die! It is all useless. A curse on Columbus! A curse on America, the thief! It is a land where the lice make fortunes, and the good men starve!"

"*Nu, nu*, Herman," my mother said gently, tying a cold towel around his head.

He felt better after supper. Some of his friends dropped in, and there was talk. His volatile mind drifted from its own troubles. Before an audience he grew talkative, and witty. Talk has ever been the joy of the Jewish race, great torrents of boundless exalted talk. Talk does not exhaust Jews as it does other people, nor give them brain-fag; it refreshes them.

Talk is the baseball, the golf, the poker, the love and the war of the Jewish race.

The whole tenement was talking and eating its supper. The broken talk came through the airshaft window. The profound bass of the East Side traffic lay under this talk. Talk. Talk. Rattle of supper dishes, whining of babies, yowling of cats; counterpoint of men, women and children talking as if their hearts would break. Talk. Jewish talk.

Even old Mrs. Fingerman's parrot talked more than other parrots. Mr. Fingerman had been an invalid for years, and his one distraction before he died had been to teach his parrot to curse in Yiddish.

As we sat at supper we could hear the parrot snarling down the airshaft at some imaginary enemy:

"Thief! Bandit! Cossack! I spit on you! A black year on you! Go into the earth! Grah! Grah! Grah!"

My father laughed heartily.

"What a good Jew that parrot is!" he said. "He can curse, and he hates Christians! I am sure we will find this parrot in the synagogue next Saturday, leading the prayers."

My father drank another glass of beer. He slammed his fist on the table, as with a sudden inspiration.

"Boys, let's go to a wine cellar to-night!" he said. "I have had a bad day, and need a little fun."

His friends agreed. To my great delight, my father took me with him. My sister protested, she wanted to come too. But my father gave her a nickel, kissed her and said: "Little girls belong with their mommas. They must be good."

2

JEWS are not drunkards; they think it is disgraceful and Christian to be heavy drinkers. But wine has been a part of Jewish life for thousands of years. There are holidays in the Jewish year when wine is brought into the synagogue, and pious old graybeards leap and dance and drink much of it, to show their joy in God.

My father rarely drank in saloons like an American. He liked his parties at home, when friends came with their women and children, and every one from grandfather down to one-year-old, drank wine, talked, and sang songs.

Wine-drinking was either religious or social. There were dozens of Russian and Roumanian wine cellars on the East Side. They were crowded with family parties after the day's work. People talked, laughed, drank wine, listened to music. That was all, no one smashed chairs about in the Christian manner, or cursed, or fought and slobbered.

Moscowitz runs a famous restaurant now on Second Avenue. In those years he kept a wine cellar on Rivington Street. It was popular among Roumanian immigrants, including my father and his friends. Mosco-

witz was, and is, a remarkable performer on the
Roumanian gypsy cymbalon.

I remember his place. It was a long narrow basement lit by gas-lamps hanging like white balloons. Between the lamps grew clusters of artificial grapes and
autumn leaves. There were many mirrors, and on
them a forgotten artist had painted scenes from Roumanian life—shepherds and sheep, a peasant, a horse
fair, peasants shocking wheat, a wedding.

At one end of the room, under a big American flag,
hung a chromo showing Roosevelt charging up San
Juan Hill. At the other end hung a Jewish Zionist flag
—blue and white bars and star of David. It draped a
crayon portrait of Dr. Theodore Herzl, the Zionist
leader, with his pale, proud face, black beard and
burning eyes. To one side was an open charcoal fire,
where lamb scallops and steaks grilled on a spit. Near
this, on a small platform, Moscowitz sat with his
cymbalon. Strings of red peppers dried in festoons
on the wall behind him. A jug of wine stood at his
elbow and after every song he poured himself a drink.

A cymbalon is a kind of zither-harp and is played
with little ebony hammers. It is unmistakably a gypsy
instrument, for the music it gives forth is soulful and
wild. As Moscowitz played, his head moved lower and
lower over the cymbalon. At the crescendo one could
not see his face, only his bald head gleaming like a
hand-mirror. Then, with a sudden upward flourish of

his arms, the music ended. One saw his shy, lean face
again, with its gray mustache. Every one cheered, applauded and whistled. Moscowitz drank off his wine,
and smiling shyly, played an encore. (Moscowitz is a
real artist, after twenty years he still makes restaurant
music with his heart, and has never saved any money.)

A hundred Jews in a basement blue as sea-fog with
tobacco smoke. The men wore their derby hats. Some
were bearded, some loud, sporty and young, some
brown as nuts. The women were fat and sweated hap-
pily, and smacked their children. Moscowitz played.
The waiters buzzed like crazy bees. A jug of the good
red Roumanian wine decorated the oilcloth on every
table. The cash register rang; Mrs. Moscowitz was
making change. The artificial grapes swung from the
ceiling. Teddy Roosevelt, with bared teeth, frightened
the Spaniards. Moscowitz played a sad and beautiful
peasant ballad. A little blubber-faced man with a red
beard beat his glass on the table, wept and sang.
Others joined him. The whole room sang.

Then talk, talk, talk again. Jewish talk. Hot, sweaty,
winey talk. A sweatshop holiday. Egypt's slaves
around the campfire in the shadow of the pyramids.
They drank wine even then. Thousands of years ago.
And talked as now. The Bible records it. And their
hearts were eased by it. And Moscowitz played the
Babylonian harp.

We sat amiably around our own jug of wine, eating

from a dish of nuts, pretzels, raisins and pickles. I drank a little wine and uttered words of wisdom.

"Pop, I like this place," I said.

My father chuckled with pride.

"Is he smart?" he asked his friends, stooping over and kissing me, so that I smelled the wine and tobacco on his mustache. "Is this boy smart, or no?" They nodded their heads solemnly, as if I were a genius.

"He will be at least a millionaire," said Mottke Blinder, smiling his broad, gentle, foolish smile that traveled from ear to ear. He was a vestmaker who was nicknamed the Blind One because he was so cross-eyed.

"No," said my father, "my Mechel must become a doctor. I will make the money for him. Learning is more precious than wealth; so it stands in the Talmud, Mottke."

"I agree with you," said Mottke, hastily, smiling again all over his gentle gargoyle's face. "Of course, Herman, but why can't he be a millionaire, too, maybe?"

I could not take my eyes off the gleaming bald head of Moscowitz, the musician.

"Pop, what song is he playing now?" I asked.

"Don't you know?" my father asked in real surprise.

"No."

"Yi! yi! yi!" my father sighed, sentimentally. "I

see, Mechel, you have really become an American.
That is the song, Mechel, the shepherds play on their
flutes in Roumania when they are watching the sheep.
It is a *doina*. How many summer days have I heard it
in the fields!"

"It is better than your American ragtime," said
Mottke severely. "It is music—not this pah-pah-pah
ragtime."

"Music of the soul," said my father sentimentally.

"Certainly," Mottke agreed.

Mottke always tried to agree with my father.
Mottke thought my father a very learned man. And
it is true that when drinking wine with his friends,
my father became unusually profound, deep, schol-
arly. He was also very witty. His talk would alternate
between ribald jokes and Talmudic epigrams and
anecdotes.

My father liked to pass himself off as a Talmud
scholar. I am sure now that he had never studied in
that strange book of medieval Jewish wisdom. The
truth is that Reb Samuel, the Chassidic umbrella-
maker in our tenement, used to tell him these things.
My father would remember, and repeat the Talmudic
tidbits on all occasions. The effect pleased his dramatic soul.

"The Talmud is the greatest book in the world,"
declared my father solemnly, as he drank another
glass of wine. "And why shouldn't it be? Wasn't it

written by the greatest rabbis in history? They took time for the work, not a week, not a month, but hundreds of years. No, they did not hurry themselves the way writers do to-day."

"Certainly not," said Mottke.

"From the Talmud one can learn anything," said my father. "For instance, it takes the Angel Gabriel six flaps of his wings to come down to earth. The Angel Simon it takes four flaps, but the Angel of Death, Mottke, him it takes only one flap of the wings. Thus it is written in the Talmud."

"Wonderful!" said Mottke. "It is wonderful to be learned."

Mendel Bum laughed raucously.

"Ha! ha!" he sneered in his hoarse, humorous voice, "you others may believe in the Talmud, but I don't! It is all grandmother stories."

"You," my father answered, with a look of deep disgust, "you, Mendel, are nothing but a bum! You sleep in parks, you beg cheese sandwiches, you sell your soul for potatoes to the Christian missionaries. What can a bum like you know of the Talmud? It was written for Jews and men, not for bums."

"Yes, Herman, but listen," Mendel began, shaken by the fury of this attack.

"Silence, Epicurean!" my father shouted, striking the table. Mendel laughed and shrugged his shoulders. He offered no further argument. He did not wish to offend my father. Mendel was living gratis at our home. He was too sensible to give up his meal-ticket for the sake of a little thing like the Talmud.

We drank wine, we cracked the walnuts between our jaws, we ate pickles and talked; talked, talked. Moscowitz played the sweet gypsy dulcimer, and a hundred Jews in derby hats filled the basement with smoke and laughter.

3

MY father made me stand on a table, to recite the poem I had learned in school:

> *I love the name of Washington,*
> *I love my country, too,*
> *I love the flag, the dear old flag,*
> *The red, white and blue.*

Horny hands applauded. A fat woman with a red, enthusiastic face gave me a pretzel. Moscowitz smiled at me and rattled his sticks across the strings of the cymbalon in approval. Some men at a table banged their glasses on the table. My father helped me down, and kissed my flushed cheeks.

"Look," said my father proudly, "did you ever hear such good English? Already he speaks English, and I am in the country ten years and can't speak a word!"

"This is a scholar!" said Mottke, patting my head

fondly. "A millionaire he could become, but it is better he should be a doctor and scholar."

Then the heat, the smoke, the excitement and wine weighed on my eyelids like lead, and I could not hold them open. I fell asleep on my father's lap, my head resting on the table.

Suddenly I was on my feet, blinking in the gaslight. Mottke held my hand, and was urging me to walk. Where was my father? Bewildered, I stared about me through the fog.

"Where is my pop?" I asked Mottke. His foolish, good-natured face was creased with disquiet. He pointed toward a table near the door. There stood my father waving his arms, and shouting at a little pock-faced man in a gray suit and derby hat. The little man was frightened. His fishy blue eyes bulged from their sockets, and were tearful with helplessness. He tried to get up, but my father pushed him back into the chair.

"Jews and friends!" my father shouted to every one around him, as he grabbed the little man by the coat, "honest Jews, look at this worm! He is a swindler, a murderer, a bloodsucker! He has tried to destroy me, to eat my flesh! Look at him! He shivers with fear, he knows I will have my revenge!"

Mendel, Aaron Katz, and several waiters were trying to persuade my father to stop his shouting. The whole wine cellar was watching. I trembled with ex·

citement, I wanted to rush to the help of my father.

But Mottke pressed my hand, and led me out into the street. My father and the others soon joined us. The men were still trying to calm my father. He shouted at them. We parted at the corner, and my father and I walked home alone. He was in a fever, and stopped to wipe his wet face.

"That thief, that Sam Kravitz!" he muttered, "why don't I kill him? He sits there so cool, so proud, so fat with the money he stole from me!"

It was a warm night; the street was crowded with people slowly walking up and down. The store windows glared with light; a few peddlers were still calling their wares. I could see the moon in the dark-blue sky over the black tenements. I felt dizzy, as if I had spent the day at Coney Island, and had stuffed on too many hot dogs.

My father stopped in front of a saloon, and stared at me in the bright electric blaze. His eyes were like burning coals. I was frightened.

"Little son," said my father in a strange, intense voice, "I am a man in a trap. All is lost unless I can borrow three hundred dollars somewhere."

"Yes, poppa."

"Promise me one thing, my sweet son."

"Yes, poppa."

"Promise that you will become a doctor."

"Yes, poppa."

"Your momma and I will work our fingers off to make you a something. You will not be a pauper and worker like your unfortunate father. We will yet show that thief, that Sam Kravitz, that he has not destroyed us!"

"Yes, poppa."

"I will make money for you; don't fear, my son. But you must study! You must not play hookey from school, or go around with that Nigger! He is a bad boy and will come to a bad end. But you must become a learned one!"

"Yes, poppa."

4

THREE hours later the tenement sleeps, the streets mutter in their sleep. Darkness, the old mother, has not forgotten my East Side. We are at peace in her womb. The pimps sleep. The cops sleep. The old Talmud dreamers sleep. The Rocky Mountains, the Atlantic Ocean, my Chrystie Street and Bronx Park are in darkness.

Sleep. I sleep and have bad dreams. I whirl through space, and fall down huge gulfs of nothingness. Then there is an explosion. Five great red stars crash all about me. . . .

I awoke with a cry. And then my mother came rushing out of the bedroom, pale as a ghost. The gas was lit. Everything in my familiar house was queer and startling, as if I were still in my nightmare.

I heard my father groaning in a strange voice. "Quick, quick, a doctor! I am dying!"

My sister woke, and cried; Mendel and my Aunt Lena woke and dressed. My aunt and I scurried for the doctor. First we rang the bell of Dr. Axelrod. He did not answer at first. We waited on the dark lonely stoop with beating hearts. Then he stuck his head out of the window, in a nightcap.

"The doctor isn't in," he mumbled grouchily. "Stop ringing that bell."

I knew it was he, but he slammed down the window before I could tell him so. My aunt and I then called the other doctor on our street, the young Dr. Solow. He came at once, bringing his little black satchel.

He examined my father and assured him he would not die. It was just indigestion and nerves. He gave my father some pills.

My father was sick for three days after seeing his cousin Sam Kravitz in the wine cellar.

CHAPTER 11

THE GANGSTER'S MOTHER

1

MANY gangsters keep pigeons, and fly them from the East Side roofs. They like to gather in bird stores on the East Side, in basements white as tombs with bird-droppings, to discuss the market in murder and pigeons. There has been a pigeon cult among New York gangsters for fifty years.

One hates gangsters, as one must hate all mercenaries. Yet some are unfortunate boys, bad eggs, hatched by the bad world hen.

Gyp the Blood, who burned in the chair for the killing of the gambler Rosenthal, was in my class at public school. He was just the ordinary rugged East Side boy. Any of us might have ended in the electric chair with him. I am not proud I escaped, it is only my luck.

I knew some gangsters well when I was sixteen. When I was a child I knew Louis One Eye, who flew pigeons on the roof next to ours.

2

LOUIS ONE EYE seized this roof and held it for his own, like a despot. The roof was important to a tenement, and so Louis was hated. In summer, when the Sun turned gangster and slugged workers and their children in the street, the roof gave us help.

Like rats scrambling on deck from the hold of a burning ship, that's how we poured on the roof at night to sleep. What a mélange in the starlight! Mothers, graybeards, lively young girls, exhausted sweatshop fathers, young consumptive coughers and spitters, all of us snored and groaned there side by side, on newspapers or mattresses. We slept in pants and undershirt, heaped like corpses. The city reared about us.

Each family was polite enough to leave a space between itself and the next family. This was our only privacy on the roof. I woke one hot choking night and saw it all like a bad dream. I saw the mounds of pale stricken flesh tossing against an unreal city. I was frightened, and didn't know where I was. Then I cried, and wondered what would happen if I jumped off the roof. My mother heard me, and soothed me, and I went back to sleep.

Sometimes the wind stirred from the Atlantic. Sometimes the hot fantastic moon looked down, and remembered us in the Arabian desert.

Some nights it rained. The heavens suddenly split, the thunder rolled down the Brooklyn Bridge. We saw the lightning, like a stroke of insanity, as it created huge nightmare vistas of an unbelievable city of towers, New York.

All sprang up in bedlam, screaming, cursing the rain, shouting to others, the babies in weak tears. We grabbed our bedding, and scrambled back into the fire of the bedrooms. But there were some who slept through the rain, rather than go back into that fire.

It is said that the Dawn is beautiful, but where? On the roof nobody loved that hour when the feverglow appeared on the pale sky, as on a consumptive's cheek. Then the swarms of bloodsucking flies arrived, and sleep was intolerable, and the humid day was here, and reality, and poverty.

Women hung their washlines on the roof. And lovers climbed there, seeking that treasure which will never be found on the East Side: privacy.

We children played on the roof. It was quieter than the street, though as dangerous. We flew kites, or explored the upper world from roof to roof, a horror for mothers to think about.

Yes, the roof was important. All roofs were social playgrounds and bedrooms, yet Louis One Eye had seized the roof of his tenement, and was master of an island of hot tin, smoky chimneys and bright gangsters' pigeons. And he was hated for it.

3

Louis was young. He had a slim, springy body, he was graceful as a snake. He had Indian hair and proud Jewish features. He would have been handsome but for his one eye, and the hard sneer fixed on his mouth. These disfigured him like wounds. They *were* the fatal wounds given him by Society.

A legend ran that Louis had a violent father. At fourteen Louis saw his father attempt to beat his mother. Louis pushed the man out of a window and almost killed him. For this the boy was sent to a reformatory.

There the State "reformed" him by carefully teaching him to be a criminal, and by robbing him of his eye.

Is there any gangster who is as cruel and heartless as the present legal State?

No. A keeper once lashed Louis for an hour with a leather belt. The boy had broken some "rule." The flying buckle cracked open an eyeball. The boy screamed in pain. But the insane and legal gangster of the State continued the "punishment."

All that night the boy lay sobbing and bleeding in his cell. He was fourteen years old. In the morning he was quiet. In the morning a cruel and legal "Doctor" of the State snipped out the useless pulp of an eye. Louis had been known as One Eye ever since.

His remaining eye had become fierce and large.
It was black, and from it poured hate, lust, scorn and
suspicion, as from a deadly headlight to shrivel the
world.

Every one feared Louis; he carried a gun. He had
killed men, and was touchy as a cat. The State had
turned a moody unhappy boy into this evil rattlesnake,
that struck a deathblow at the slightest touch of man.

He had built a large coop for his pigeons, and
twice a day let them out to fly. We watched him
secretly from behind a chimney. He stood on a cor-
nice, sinister against the sky. From other roofs, other
quadrilles of pigeons were wheeling and maneuvering,
as though it were a heartbreaking joy. They seemed so
free and beautiful, we envied them.

But then Louis One Eye waved his long bamboo
pole. He whistled the long mysterious signal known to
pigeon fanciers. From the glimmering sky the pigeons
descended like a heavenly chain gang, and returned
meekly to their prison. They were not free. We children always marveled at this, but now the secret is
known to me; pigeons, like men, are easily tamed with
food.

4

AT that time I was in love with my Aunt Lena. It was
painful, when we walked down the street, that men
stared familiarly after my Aunt Lena, and winked,

and tried to pinch her legs, or said nasty things. And I couldn't fight back. Once a pimp grabbed her arm and tried to kiss her. She slapped his face, and made a cop laugh.

There were always men about. A fresh young girl is marked anywhere, she creates a fever, she is a magnet. Life has been drab or hopeless, and then she comes, like a false Messiah, and even the brutes dream.

Klemm the Ox, a young German baker who worked on our street, brought her a baker's homage of new rolls every morning. He stole these at his job. Aaron Katz the cloakmaker took her to the Yiddish vaudeville theaters. Louis One Eye caught me watching him at his pigeon flying one dusk. He didn't wallop me, to my surprise, but what was worse, asked questions about my Aunt Lena.

5

SHE had arrived from Hungary, in a dark hour, in a bad winter. My father was out of a job, my mother exhausted with worries. It had snowed for weeks. The slush filled the streets like wet poison, all of us were miserable with colds. On every street there was an eviction; my father groaned, "our turn is next."

But my Aunt Lena was not affected by all this. She was sixteen years old, and it was her first great adventure, this immigration. She was happy when she first came.

Who could help loving the beautiful little "greenhorn" girl? She had rosy peasant cheeks, and shiny black hair that was her pride, and that she spent hours braiding as she sang. She was formed like a woman, but her eyes were a child's, they were so clear, pure of guile, and happy.

She chattered about our house, her eyes glowed, she clapped her hands like a delighted baby. How crazy she was about America, about the common things we knew so well! The language, the big houses, the people, everything fascinated her. She could scarcely sleep for excitement when she first arrived. She sprang out of bed, and sang as she cooked the breakfast, waking us all. She wanted to be off. Breakfast over, she put on her red Hungarian shawl, and set forth on the second discovery of America.

Sometimes she took me along. We walked all over the city, from the Battery to Central Park. We rode the glorious horsecars, we marveled at the dignity of the people on Fifth Avenue. We watched the busy little tugboats on the East River, we shared in the pushcart battles on Orchard Street.

Everything was wonderful to my Aunt Lena. But my mother feared for her. The pimps hunted for beautiful greenhorn girls, she might be kidnaped or lost. But my Aunt Lena was afraid of nothing, she

laughed and all of us laughed with her. She was so
happy at first, it made us all happy.

Then everything came to an end.

6

ONE night at supper, my mother said:

"Lena, listen."

"Yes, Katie."

"Lena, what's to be done? We can't pay the rent
again."

"No?" said my Aunt Lena in alarm.

"Little sister, we're poor. If I didn't have to cook
and sew and take care of the children, I'd look for a
job. Don't you think you could begin to work, Lena?"

My Aunt Lena looked up in surprise.

"Me, Katie?" she said, her lips curling mournfully
like a child's. "Must I work? In the old country I
didn't work!"

"No," said my mother, "but here we're poor, sister.
Here we have no cows and chickens as in Hungary.
Here every one works, even the children."

"But I want to see things, Katie!"

My Aunt Lena looked as if she were about to cry.
It made me sad, too, I could scarcely eat my goulash.
Then she laughed.

"Katie, I'm foolish," my aunt said. "Of course I'll
work. I'll work by day, and then at night, I can still

see things. I'll go to the river at night to see the boats, won't I, Katie?"

"Yes, little sister, at night you will see the boats," said my mother quietly.

So my Aunt Lena went to work in a clothing shop, where the youth, the charm and ecstasy of the East Side were buried then. The routine changed her. She was tired at night, and had to wash and iron her blouses for the next day, and do many other things. After that we rarely went to see the tugboats work on the river, or the pushcarts on Orchard Street, and the other sights of America.

7

BUT there were the men always calling at our house. It kept me in a state of anxiety.

"Aunt Lena," I said, "you'll be sure to marry me when I grow up, won't you?"

"Yes, Mikey, dear, it's you I'll marry."

"Do you swear it?"

"Yes, see, Mikey, I kiss my little finger and swear it. You'll grow up and be a famous rich doctor, and then I'll marry you. You, only you, Mikey!"

She kissed me, and my heart beat wildly. A new body was waking, that was to live its hour on earth, a mystery in feeling and pain.

8

ONCE my Aunt Lena lay sick in our bedroom. There
had been a rush season in the shop, and she had
worked too hard. The sweatshops were run on piece-
work then, a system of Egyptian slavery under which
the strongest crumpled, as though it were the bubonic
plague.

My aunt's face was pale, her beautiful eyes were
languid with pain. She smiled and kissed me when I
came from school.

"Mickey," she said, "after you eat your coffee and
butter-bread, I want you to do something for me."

"Yes, Aunt Lena."

"Here is ten cents. I want you to go to the music
store, and get the words of these songs for me. And I
will sing them, and we will forget piece-work."

She had written the names on an old envelope; my
aunt had quickly learned English. I ate my afternoon
lunch, and went to the music store, and brought her
the song sheets.

I always loved to hear her sing. I sat there, while
she stroked my hair, and was filled with a painful
delight. My mother came from the kitchen to listen,
too. My aunt explained those songs to her.

One was called "She's Only a Bird in a Gilded
Cage." It was the story, my aunt said, of a poor girl
who had married a rich man to help her family. But

she regretted the slavery and hypocrisy this brought, and grew sadder and sadder, and died.

My mother shook her head in sympathy, and said, in Yiddish: "Alas, alas! How pitiful!"

The other song, I remember, was called "The Rabbi's Daughter."

It was the story of a stern, upright old Rabbi whose daughter fell in love with a Christian youth, and married him. Her heartbroken father performed the awful Hebrew rite in such cases; he held a funeral service for her.

He tried to forget, but could not. So he, too, grew sadder and sadder, and died of grief. Then his daughter grew sadder and sadder and died for grief of him.

My mother shook her head again, and tears were in her eyes.

"*Ai*, how sad that is, how sad and beautiful!" she said. "It is just like life."

I look back at that moment. I know a cynic or a Broadway clown must have written those songs, with tongue in cheek, maybe, for money. It is sophisticated to laugh at such songs. But I remember my Aunt Lena, sickened by piece-work slavery in the shop, singing them in her deep voice, I remember my mother's tears.

9

ABOUT that time a grocery storekeeper was shot by some cheap young thieves a few blocks away. It was in all the papers. I heard whispering among the indignant neighbors that Louis One Eye's gang had done the job.

Then a child was raped in a cellar, a poor little screaming girl.

Then some one set off a bomb in an Italian's house. We heard the boom one night; it started a panic. We scuttled down in our underwear at three in the morning. The tenement had rocked; the street was crowded with mad-eyed people in underwear; it was like the Day of Judgment.

It was only the Black Hand again, but the neighbors whispered it was Louis One Eye.

They blamed everything on Louis. He didn't care. He swaggered about, and pushed people off the sidewalks as if he were a king. He never had a friendly word for any one. Some of his thieving was open as a politician's. He forced storekeepers to buy tickets to imaginary picnics and dances. He ate fruit off pushcarts and didn't pay, as calmly as though he were a cop.

The neighbors hated him, they wanted the janitor to force him to move out with his pigeons.

The fat janitor was very profound about the matter. "You can't make him move; you can't touch Louis," said the janitor sagely. "Louis is under the protection of Tammany Hall."

He never worked, of course; he went to jail several

times; he was a bad egg. Even if you felt strong, you couldn't afford to fight him; for he had a gun. And even if you grabbed his gun, and beat him up, his gang would get you in the end. He ruled the tenement; and all hated him, and blamed him for everything.

His old mother, half-crippled, hunched in an old shawl, like some humble dwarf, alone loved Louis. She hobbled about, and on the street and in the grocery store, would stop people and stare into their faces with her dim eyes, and ask: "Why do they say my Louis is a bad boy? My Louis is a good boy. Why can't they leave him alone? My Louis is a good boy."

Louis must have loved his mother, too; he helped her up the stairs; he shopped mornings for the groceries, to save her rheumatic legs the pain of walking; he gave her money every week, and bought her dresses.

Once there was an Italian *festa* a few blocks away. The lamps were lit in arches between the tenements; a band played; chestnuts and candy were on sale; the Italians pinned dollar bills on the shrine of their saint.

Suddenly there was a riot, and I saw Louis, single-handed, beat up three Italian roughnecks who had pulled the beard of a frightened old Jew who had wandered like ourselves into that Christian land.

10

ONE hot night, after work, my Aunt Lena and I climbed on the roof for air. My aunt was in her kimono. She had just washed her long, black hair, it hung down her back. No one was on the roof but Louis; he was flying his pigeons in the hot twilight.

When I saw him, I was frightened. I wanted to go back. My Aunt Lena reassured me. We spread newspapers as far away from him as possible, and sat down.

He saw us out of his single eye. My heart beat as he walked over slowly, a gleam in his big eye. I think he tried to smile, but that sneer was not to be wiped out so easily.

"Hey, kid," he said to my aunt, "come over here and lookit my pigeons."

I could feel my Aunt Lena stiffen; now she was getting frightened.

Louis came nearer. "Listen," he said, out of the corner of his sneering mouth, "I got some fine pigeons, kiddo. I got a fantail worth ten dollars, and six rubies I pulled down from another guy's flock on Forsythe Street. He tried to shoot me for them."

Louis bent over, and touched my aunt's hair with his hot stubby hand. She sat there paralyzed.

"Run along, Mike, I want to talk to your aunt."

I stared at him. I couldn't move. In a moment I

felt that I would fling myself at his legs, bite them, do
anything to save my aunt. He put his hands on my
aunt's kimono, and tried to tear it open. She sprang
up, screaming, and clawed at his face with her nails.
He grabbed her. I ran to the roof door and yelled
down the hallway.

Suddenly, I don't know how or why, the roof was
filled with all the neighbors. I don't know how they
came so soon, crowds always sprang up on the East
Side like dynamite explosions.

The mob of neighbors faced Louis. He backed up
against his pigeon coop in surprise.

"What happened?" Morris, a husky young clothing worker asked. My aunt told them. They glared at
Louis threateningly. But he had gotten his nerve back.
Before she was through explaining, he began pushing
the crowd.

"Get off my roof!" he snarled, his face hateful as
a gorilla's.

The crowd moved away slowly, muttering. Suddenly some one in back threw an old wooden box at
Louis. It hit him in the face. A projecting nail tore a
gash under his one eye, and it bled.

Louis frothed like a madman, he raged up and
down.

"Who done that?" he screamed, pulling out his
gun. "I'll kill the bastard who done it." We watched

him frozen with horror, as we might an escaped madman.

Then, from somewhere, his old mother appeared.
She hobbled up to her son, and looked at him with her
dim, patient eyes.

"Are you hurt, Louis?" she said, feebly. "Why are
you bothering my Louis?" she asked the neighbors.
"My Louis is a good boy, he doesn't harm any one."

She hadn't even seen his gun. Louis slipped it into
his pocket, and patted her on the back.

"It's all right, momma," he said, "go back in the
house."

She took a handkerchief, and wiped the blood from
his eye, mumbling complaints against the bad world.
The neighbors drifted away, looking a little ashamed,
as if they were in the wrong. And Louis's pigeons, that
he had neglected all this time, flew down in a great
whir of wings on their coop, prisoners, like all of us,
of the East Side.

Every one went on hating Louis One Eye, and I did
too. Now I hate more those who took an East Side boy
and turned him into a monster useful to bosses in
strikes, and to politicians on election day.

CHAPTER 12

MUSHROOMS IN BRONX PARK

1

THE summer. It was painful to draw one's breath. The sun blazed with sheer murder all day. At night, steam rose from the ghetto stones like a Russian vapor bath. There was never any relief from the weight pressing on our necks and skulls. People were sick, doctors were busy.

The Jewish babies whimpered and died. The flies thrived. Every one was nervous; there were quarrels down the airshaft. I would wake in the dead of night and hear the tenement groaning and twisting in bedrooms. People went exploring for sleep as for a treasure. Hollow-eyed ghosts tramped the streets all night. Families slept on the docks, in the parks, on the roofs. But the world was hot.

2

SOME nights my mother laid bedding on the sidewalk before our tenement. While she and my father fanned themselves on the stoop and gossiped with the neighbors, my sister and I slept in the street.

The street cars, the wagons, the talk, the sudden shrieks, the million shoes of passers-by grinding like

141

an emery wheel on the pavements did not disturb our
sleep. But one night something did happen that left a
permanent mark on my mind.

It was the evening before the Fourth of July. There
was the usual debauch of patriotism Kids were shooting off toy cannons, firecrackers and their fingers in
every street. The night was lit with a city's bombard-
ment. Grinning Italians shot their revolvers at the
sky. Roman candles popped red, blue and yellow
balls at the sky. Pinwheels whirled, Catherine wheels
fizzed and turned, torpedoes crackled, and rockets
flew like long golden winged snakes above the tenements. It was fun. But I tired at last and fell asleep
on the bedding spread by my mother in front of the
tenement.

I had slept an hour, when some careless person
threw a lighted cannon cracker out of a window. It
exploded on the pillow beside my face. I leaped up
with a scream of fright, and ran to my mother. I
trembled and sobbed, and saw my blood stream. A big
slice of flesh had been torn from my left shoulder; I
still bear the scar.

This shattered meat healed quickly; the blood was
soon forgotten. What remained was the nightmare. For
weeks after that Fourth of July I woke every night,
with a scream. I was re-living the explosion. My parents did not know what to do. The fat and cheerful
Dr. Axelrod gave me pink pills to take. They did not

help. The thin and gloomy young Dr. Solow mumbled something about sending me to the country. But was that possible, my parents asked? So he gave me greenish medicine to take. It did not help.

I was losing weight. My mother took the advice of a neighbor and called in a Speaker-woman, Baba Sima the witch-doctor. It was she who cured me.

3

There were many such old women on the East Side. They were held in great respect. The East Side worshiped doctors, but in nervous cases, or in mishaps of the personal life, it sometimes reverted to medievalism.

Lovers sought philters of the old Babas, to win a victory over a rival in love. Deserted wives paid these women money to model little wax figures of their wandering husbands and torture them until the false one returned.

Baba Sima called one summer night, as I lay pale and exhausted by the dark mental shadows. She was a humpbacked old crone in a kerchief and apron, with red rheumy eyes, and protruding belly. Her flabby mouth was devoid of teeth. It was sunk so deeply that her nose and chin almost met. She was dressed as poorly as any old synagogue beggar. She sniffled and panted after the climb upstairs, and my mother gave her tea. She talked a bit, took a pinch of snuff, then waddled into the bedroom to look at me.

"*Nu, nu,*" she said, cheerfully, wiping her nose and sweaty face with a rag out of her mysterious satchel, "if it was only a firecracker, I can cure him. The boy has been frightened, but I will pass the fright away. He will be sound in a few weeks, with God's help."

She turned me on my stomach, and with a blunt knife traced magic designs on my bare back, mumbling over and over in singsong:

> "*Tanti beovati,*
> *Tanti sabatanu.*
> *Tanti Keeliati,*
> *Tanti lamachtanu.*"

"To him, and to her, and to us, and to it! The serpent and the fire, the ocean and the sun! God is Jehovah, and Jehovah is God! Rushyat! Cushyat! Cum! Tum! Sum!"

She rubbed my back lightly with a pungent oil, and wiped her hands. The first treatment was over. My mother paid her a dollar and invited her to more tea. The old lady grew amazingly greedy; she drank four glasses of tea heaped high with my mother's best rose-leaf jam. She gobbled at least a dozen butter cookies. Then she sniffled off to her next call.

I was left irritable and skeptical. This foreign hocus-pocus did not appeal to me, an American boy. I was ashamed of it. I feared the boys in my gang would hear of it, and would tease me. My mother stroked my hair.

"My dear," said my mother, "no one will tease you. Don't you want to be cured of your fright? It isn't good to be frightened in this world, one can't go through life with a fright. One is not a man. This is a famous Speaker; your poppa knew her in Roumania. She knows more than many Doctors. She learned her wisdom from a famous Zaddik. She is sure to make you well."

The next visit Baba Sima went through the same ritual and drank another gallon of tea with dozens of cookies. The third visit she left a prescription. My mother was to walk through the pushcart market on Orchard Street, and buy a glass at the first pushcart selling household things. She was forbidden to bargain, but to pay the first price the peddler demanded. The same night, I was to take this glass to the East River. If there was a moon, I was to drink a glass of river water; no moon, two glasses. Then I was to throw the glass into the river, and repeat the words: Cum, tum, sum.

I did this. On the fourth visit the Magic-Maker prescribed a paste of horse-droppings gathered in the street; mixed with a spider's web, honey, grits, thyme, my own urine, and pepper. This was smeared on my forehead for a week.

On the fourth visit the Magic-Maker brought many

things in her bag. She set them out in the kitchen; a little tin pail, a ladle, and some lead. She melted the lead over our kitchen stove, muttering weird rhymes. Then she poured the lead from the melting ladle into the pail. The lead hissed and steamed as it dropped into the water. As it cooled, it took on jagged outlines. The Magic-Maker regarded the lead long and painfully. Her toothless jaws worked; her eyes watered as if she were crying. She took many pinches of snuff.

"It is a horse!" she announced triumphantly at last. Our family group, watching her fearfully in the gaslight, was startled. "Give me another glass of tea; my cure is done, it is a horse!"

We stared at the chunk of jagged lead. Yes, we assured each other in amazement, it had taken on the shape of a horse. And the next night, exactly at midnight, my father led me into the livery stable, and I whispered into the ear of one of the coach horses:

"My fright in your body; God is Jehovah," I said, giving the horse an apple which he munched sleepily. "Cum! Tum! Sum!"

Thus I was cured. The nightmare did not return. I woke no longer screaming in the night. Yet I was skeptical, and could not believe in the magic. I asked Vassa the stable-hand whether the horse now woke at night, screaming. He said the horse didn't. But I was cured. That greedy, dirty, foolish old woman knew some deep secrets, evidently. She had cured me. I never told my friends, I was too ashamed. But I marveled that summer, and not even my parents could explain it all. They had not heard of the greater magic: Suggestion.

4

AFTER I was cured, our family life went back to its normal summer routine. My father left us mornings for his work, my mother cooked and baked, my sister Esther played jacks and skipped the rope with her girls. I played with my own gang, I fought, stole apples, read Buffalo Bill stories, went swimming, watched the prostitutes. At night my father told fairy-tales to his admiring friends, and we drank beer. Then we searched for sleep on the roof, or on the sidewalks. The world was hot.

Every Sunday morning in summer my father itched to be off somewhere. He did not want to stay in town on his one free day. But my mother hated trips. When he rode to Coney Island to swim in the ocean my mother never went along. She hated the pushing and excitement of a million frantic people.

"It's a madhouse," she grumbled. "Why must I fight a lot of hooligans because it is Sunday? I can rest better sitting here on my own stoop."

She made my father angry. He loved swimming; he could swim way out beyond the lifelines. And he loved, too, as much as I did, the razzle-dazzle, the mechanical blare, the gaudy savage joys of Coney Island.

"But the fare is cheap, only a nickel," he said. "Where else can one go for a nickel?"

"I don't care," said my mother, "it's a madhouse. Coney Island is a place for monkeys."

"Bah!" my father sneered. "You are an old Baba grandmother. You would like to sit by the stove all your life!"

"No," said my mother, calmly, "in Hungary I went to places. I used to walk there in the fields and the woods. But Coney Island is different. It has no fields."

"*Nu*," said my father, irritably, "let us go to the fields then. I will take you to Bronx Park next Sunday."

"Has it a forest there?" asked my mother.

"Yes, it has a forest," said my father.

"*Nu*, we will see then," said my mother, casually, "maybe I will go."

She was not enthusiastic. My mother had the peasant's aversion to travel. In her Hungarian village no one ever traveled far, except to America. The East Side was her village now, and she saw no reason for leaving it even on Sunday. She still lives on the East Side, on the same street, in the same tenement, an unhurried peasant. She has never been out of New York City. There are millions of such peasants in New York.

5.

SUNDAY came. My mother had evidently decided to make the trip to Bronx Park. She rose at six to get things ready. She ironed a dress for Esther, a waist for me; she darned our stockings, and packed a lunch of salami sandwiches, pickles, cake, oranges and hard-boiled eggs. Then she swept the house, cooked breakfast, and woke us.

"Stand up!" she said, yanking off our bedclothes.

"Why so early?" my father groaned sleepily.

"We are gong to Bronx Park," said my mother. "Have you forgotten?"

At breakfast my sister and I were crazy with excitement over the trip. My mother had to slap us. She was flustered and grumbly; the thought of travel confused her.

In the elevated train her face flushed purple with heat and bewilderment. No wonder; the train was worse than a cattle car. It was crowded with people to the point of nausea. Excited screaming mothers, fathers sagging under enormous lunch baskets, children yelling, puking and running under every one's legs, an old graybeard fighting with the conductor, a gang of tough Irish kids in baseball suits who persisted in swinging from the straps—sweating bodies and exasperated nerves—grinding lurching train, sudden stops when a hundred bodies battered into each other, bedlam of legs and arms, sneezing, spitting, cursing, sighing—a super-tenement on wheels.

Northward to the Bronx! And at every station new mobs of frenzied sweating families loaded with lunch baskets and babies burst through the doors. There was no room for them, but they made it for themselves by standing on our feet.

My father cursed each time a fat wet matron flopped in his lap or trod on his corns.

This was New York on Sunday. All the trains and street cars were crowded like this. Seven million people rushing to find a breath of fresh air! *"Pfui!"* said my father.

"In Roumania it is a little walk to the country," he said. "Here is is a fight for one's life. What a crazy land!"

But my mother became happier as the train rolled on. She leaned out of the window and smiled. In the streets below, the solid palisades of tenement had disappeared. There were small houses, each set among green weedy lots, and there were trees.

"It's a pleasure to see green things again," she said. "Look, another tree! I am glad we came, Herman! When we come to Bronx Park I will take off my shoes and walk in the grass. I haven't done it for fifteen years."

"They will arrest you," snarled my father, as he glared at the fat Jewish woman standing next to him, who persisted in grabbing him around the neck each time the train lurched.

"I want to pick daisies!" cried my little sister.

"Yes, yes, my darling," said my mother, fondly, "daisies and mushrooms, too. I will show you how to find mushrooms. It is more fun than picking daisies."

6

AT last the Bronx Park! My father bought us popcorn to eat, and red balloons. Then we walked through some green fields. My mother sighed as she sniffed the fragrant air.

"Ach," said my happy mother, "it's like Hungary! There is much room, and the sky is so big and blue! One can breathe here!"

So we walked until we came to a menagerie. Here we saw a gang of crazy monkeys in a cage. They were playing tag. We fed them peanuts and watched them crack open the shells. Then we saw a lion, two tigers, a white bear, some snakes, birds, and an elephant. All of them we gave peanuts.

Then we walked far into a big lonesome country. It had a big field with no one in it. It had a forest at one end. We looked for signs: KEEP OFF THE GRASS. There were no signs. So we walked into the middle of the field, and found a wonderful tree. This tree we made our own.

We spread newspapers under the tree, and my

mother laid out the lunch. We were hungry after our long ride and walk. So we ate the salami sandwiches and other good things.

My father drank two bottles of beer. Then he stretched on his back, smoked his pipe, and looked at the sky. He sang Roumanian shepherd songs. Then he fell asleep, and snored.

My mother cleaned away the newspapers. Then she looked to see if no policeman was near. There was no policeman. So she took off her shoes and stockings and walked around on the grass.

My sister and I left her and went hunting for daisies. We found some and brought them to her. She wove for us two daisy crowns out of them, the sort children wear in Hungary.

Then my mother took our hands. "Come," she said, in a whisper, "while poppa sleeps we will go into the forest and hunt mushrooms."

My father heard the whisper. His snores abruptly ended.

"Don't get lost," he mumbled, not opening his sleepy eyes.

"Pooh," said my mother, "lost in a forest? Me?"

"All right," said my father, turning on his side and snoring again.

7

IN the forest everything suddenly became cool and green. It was like going into a mysterious house. The trees were like walls, their leaves made a ceiling. Clear, sweet voices sang through the house. These were the birds. The birds lived in the house. Little ants and beetles ran about under our feet. They lived on the floor of the house.

I smelled queer, garlicky smells. I saw a large gold coin lying in a bed of green. I looked closer, and knew I was fooled. It was sunlight. The sun made other golden lines and circles. I heard running water.

My mother walked in front of us. Her face looked younger. She stopped mysteriously every few minutes, and sniffed the air.

"I am smelling out the mushrooms," she explained. "I know how to do that. I learned it in Hungary. Each mushroom has its own smell. The best ones grow under oak trees."

"I want to pick some," said Esther.

"No!" said my mother, sharply, "you must never do that. You are an American child, and don't know about these things. Some mushrooms are poison! They will kill you! Never pick them!"

"Do they come on strings?" I asked.

"Those are the grocery store mushrooms," explained my mother. "Ach, America, the thief, where children only see dry, dead mushrooms in grocery stores! Wait, I will show you!"

There was a flush of excitement on her black, gypsy face. We were surprised at our mother. She was always so slow-moving and careful. Now she jumped over big rocks and puddles and laughed like a girl.

"Stop! I think there are mushrooms under those leaves!" she said. "Let me scratch a little and find out. Yes, yes! do you see? My nose is still sharp after all these years! What a pretty silver cap it has! It is a birch mushroom. Its parents are those birch trees. When mushrooms grow near pine trees they are green, and taste of pine. But the oak mushroom is the finest of all. It is a beautiful brown."

She broke off pieces of the mushroom for us to nibble. "It is better with salt," she said. "But how good it is! It is not like the rubbish they grow here in cellars! No, the American mushrooms have no worth. They taste and look like paper. A real mushroom should taste of its own earth or tree. In Hungary we know that!"

We followed her, as she poked around under the trees and bushes for her beloved mushrooms. She found many, and lifted her skirt to make a bag for them. Each new mushroom reminded her of Hungary and of things she had never told us. She talked in a low, caressing voice. She stooped to the mushrooms, and her eyes shone like a child's.

"Ach, how people love the mushrooms in Hungary! In the season every one is in the forest with a big basket to hunt. We had our own favorite spots where we went year after year. We never plucked mushrooms, but cut them close to the roots, like this. It means they will grow again next year. Two other Jewish girls and I always went hunting together."

"Momma, can mushrooms talk to each other?"

"Some people say so. Some people say that at night mushrooms not only talk, but dance with each other. They turn into jolly old men with beards. In the morning they become mushrooms again.

"Birds talk to each other, too, people say. I used to know the names of all the birds, and their songs. I knew good snakes and bad, and killed the bad ones with a stick. I knew where to find blueberries and huckleberries. I could walk twenty miles in a forest and find my way back. Once, two girls and I were lost in a forest for days and found our way back. Ach, what fun there was in Hungary!"

Suddenly my mother flung her arms around each of us, and kissed Esther and me.

"Ach, Gott!" she said, "I'm so happy in a forest! You American children don't know what it means! I am happy!"

~~~~~~

CHAPTER 13

JEWS AND CHRISTIANS

1

MY mother never learned to like shoes. In Hungary, in her native village, she had rarely worn them, and she could see no reason for wearing them here.

"Does one wear shoes on one's hands?" she would ask. "How can one work in shoes? Shoes are only for people to show off in."

So she paddled about in bare feet whenever she could. This annoyed my father at those times when he was ambitious. To him not wearing shoes was like confessing to the world that one was poor. But my mother had no such false pride, and would even walk barefooted in the street.

Once my father bought her a diamond ring on the installment plan. It was during one of his periods of greatness, when he had earned a big week's pay, and the Boss had hinted at a foreman's job for him.

It was on a Saturday night, and he had been drinking beer with his fellow-workmen. He came home flushed and dramatic. With many flourishes and the hocus-pocus of a magician he extracted the ring from his vest pocket and placed it on my mother's finger.

"At last, Katie!" he said, kissing her with great ceremony, "at last you have a diamond ring! At last you can write home to Hungary that you too are wearing diamonds in America!"

"Pouf!" said my mother angrily, pushing him away. She snatched the ring from her finger as if it burned her. "What foolishness!"

"Foolishness!" my father exclaimed, indignantly. "What! it is foolish to wear diamonds?"

"Yes," said my stubborn mother.

"Every one wears diamonds!" said my father, "every one with a little pride."

"Let others be proud! I am a work horse," said my mother.

My father spat in disgust, and stalked off to find some intelligent males.

The ring remained in the family. It was our only negotiable capital. It was hidden among some towels and sheets in the bureau. In time of need it traveled to the pawnshop, to buy us food and rent. Many East Side families aspired to jewelry for this reason. Money vanished. Jewelry remained. This was the crude credit system of the East Side.

2

MY mother was fond of calling herself a work horse. She was proud of the fact that she could work hard. She wanted no diamond rings, no fancy dresses, no decorations. She had a strong sense of reality, and felt that when one was poor, only strength could help one. But my father was a romantic, and dreamed of a bright easy future.

My humble funny little East Side mother! How can I ever forget this dark little woman with bright eyes, who hobbled about all day in bare feet, cursing in Elizabethan Yiddish, using the forbidden words "ladies" do not use, smacking us, beating us, fighting with her neighbors, helping her neighbors, busy from morn to midnight in the tenement struggle for life.

She would have stolen or killed for us. She would have let a railroad train run over her body if it could have helped us. She loved us all with the fierce painful love of a mother-wolf, and scolded us continually like a magpie.

Mother! Momma! I am still bound to you by the cords of birth. I cannot forget you. I must remain faithful to the poor because I cannot be faithless to you! I believe in the poor because I have known you. The world must be made gracious for the poor! Momma, you taught me that!

3

WHAT a hard life she had led. She had known nothing but work since her tenth year. Her father had died then, and she was the oldest child of a large family. She went to work in a bakery, then did a man's labor on a farm.

When she was eighteen, relatives gathered seventy-five gulden, and sent her to America as the last hope for her family. She was to work here and send for her brothers and sisters.

The crossing made a deep mark on her mind. She spent seventeen agonized days in the filthy steerage, eating nothing but herrings and potatoes, because there was no *kosher* food.

Her first night in America was spent amid groans and confusion on the floor of a crowded cellar for immigrants. It was called the Nigger House.

A relative found her the next morning. He took her to a job. It was in an East Side restaurant where she was paid five dollars a month, with meals. She slept on a mattress in the evil, greasy kitchen. The working hours were from five to midnight.

In a year she saved enough money to send a ship ticket to her oldest brother.

"Yes, I have had all kinds of good times in America," she would chuckle grimly, when she told us of this time. "Yes, that first year in the restaurant I had lots of fun with the pots and pans.

"It's lucky I'm alive yet. It is a good land, but not for the poor. When the Messiah comes to America, he had better come in a fine automobile, with a dozen servants. If he comes here on a white horse, people will think he is just another poor immigrant. They may set him to work washing dishes in a restaurant."

4

SHE and my father had married in the old Jewish style; that is, they were brought together by a professional matrimonial broker. He charged them a commission for the service. It is as good a method as any. My parents came to love each other with an emotion deeper than romance; I am sure my father would have died for my mother. But she also made his head ache, and he told her so often.

She was a buttinsky. She tried to "reform" everybody, and fought people because they were "bad." She spoke her mind freely, and told every one exactly where the path of duty lay. She was always engaged in some complicated ethical brawl, and my father had to listen to all the details.

Or she was always finding people in trouble who needed her help. She helped them for days, weeks and months, with money, food, advice and the work of her hands.

She was a midwife in many hasty births, a nurse in sickness, a peacemaker in family battles.

She knew how to make a poultice for boils by chewing bread and mixing it with yellow soap; and how to cure colds with kerosene, and the uses of herbs and

other peasant remedies. She was a splendid cook and
breadmaker, and shared all these secrets with the
neighbors.

When a woman fell sick, the distracted husband
appealed to my mother; and for weeks she'd drop in
there twice a day, to cook the meals, and scrub the
floors, and bathe the children, to joke, gossip, scold,
love, to scatter her strength and goodness in the dark
home.

It would have shocked her if any one had offered
to pay for these services. It was simply something that
had to be done for a neighbor.

Once there was a woman on our street who was
going crazy. Her cigarmaker husband had deserted
her and two children. The woman had spells, and
could not sleep at night. She begged my mother to
sleep with her. She was afraid she would kill her
children during one of her spells.

So my mother slept there every night for more than
a month.

How often have I seen my mother help families
who were evicted because they could not pay rent.
She wrapped herself in her old shawl, and went begging through the tenements for pennies. Puffing with
bronchitis, she dragged herself up and down the steep
landings of a hundred tenements, telling the sad tale
with new emotion each time and begging for pennies.

But this is an old custom on the East Side; whenever

a family is to be evicted, the neighboring mothers put on their shawls and beg from door to door.

5

MY poor father, worrying over his own load of American troubles, had to listen to the tremendous details of all these tragedies. My mother could discover so many sick people! And so many bad people who needed to be fought! No wonder my father drank beer! No wonder he grabbed his head between his hands, and groaned:

"Stop! you give me a headache! I can't listen any more!"

"It is not your head, but your selfishness!" scoffed my mother.

"One has to be selfish in America," said my father. "It is dog eat dog over here. But you, you neglect your own family to help every passing stranger."

"*Pfui,* what a lie!" my mother spat. "When have my children been neglected?"

"But for God's sake," said my father, "haven't we enough troubles of our own? You're like a man with consumption. It is not enough for him to have this, he has to go skating so that he can break his leg, too."

"*Nu,* I can stand a broken leg," said my mother. "What is a leg when there is so much misery in the world?"

6

My mother was opposed to the Italians, Irish, Germans and every other variety of Christian with whom we were surrounded.

"May eight and eighty black years fall on these *goys!*" she said, her black eyes flashing. "They live like pigs; they have ruined the world. And they hate and kill Jews. They may seem friendly to us to our faces, but behind our backs they laugh at us. I know them well. I have seen them in Hungary."

My father sat one evening at the supper table, drinking beer and reading a Yiddish newspaper. In the hot kitchen my mother was washing the dishes, and humming a Hungarian folk song.

"*Nu, nu!*" my father exclaimed, striking the table with his fist, "another railroad accident! Katie, I have always said it is dangerous to travel on these American railroads!"

"What has happened?" my mother gasped, appearing from the kitchen with steaming hands and face.

"What has happened, you ask?" my father repeated in the important tone of a pedant. "What has happened is that seventeen innocent people were killed in a railroad accident in New Jersey! And whose fault was it? The fault of the rich American railroads!"

My mother was horrified. She wiped her boiling

face with her apron and muttered: "God help us and shield us! Were there any Jews among the dead?"

My father glanced rapidly through the list of names. "No," he said, "only Christians were killed."

My mother sighed with relief. She went back into her kitchen. She was no longer interested; Christians did not seem like people to her. They were abstractions. They were the great enemy, to be hated, feared and cursed. In Hungary three Christian peasant girls had once taunted her. Then they had gone in swimming, and had been drowned. This was God's punishment on them for persecuting a Jew. Another peasant had once plucked the beard of an old reverend Jew, and God struck him with lightning a week later. My mother was full of such anecdotes.

The East Side never forgot Europe. We children heard endless tales of the pogroms. Joey Cohen, who was born in Russia, could himself remember one. The Christians had hammered a nail into his uncle's head, and killed him. When we passed a Christian church we were careful to spit three times; otherwise bad luck was sure to befall us. We were obsessed by wild stories of how the Christians loved to kidnap Jewish children, to burn a cross on each cheek with a redhot poker. They also cut off children's ears, and made a kind of soup. Nigger had once seen Jewish ears for sale in the window of a Christian butcher shop.

"In the old days," my mother said, "the Christians hunted the Jews like rabbits. They would gather thousands in a big marketplace, and stuff pork down their throats with swords, and ask the Jews to be baptized. The Jews refused, of course. So they were burnt in great fires, and the Christians laughed, danced and made merry when they saw the poor Jews burning up like candles. Such are the Christians. May they burn some day, too."

These impressions sank into my heart, and in my bad dreams during the hot summer nights, dark Christian ogres the size of tenements moved all around me. They sat on my chest, and clutched my throat with slimy remorseless fingers, shrieking, "Jew, Jew! Jew!"

And I would spend long daylight hours wondering why the Christians hated us so, and form noble plans of how I would lead valiant Jewish armies when I grew up, in defense of the Jews.

7

BUT my mother was incapable of real hatred. Paradoxically she had many warm friends among the Italian and Irish neighbors. She was always apologetic about this. "These are not like other Christians," she would say, "these are good people." How could she resist another human being in trouble? How could she be indifferent when another was in pain?

Her nature was made for universal sympathy, without thought of prejudice. Her hatred of Christians was really the outcry of a motherly soul against the boundless cruelty in life.

Betsy was an Italian woman who lived in the next tenement. She had a long, emaciated face covered with moles, engraved with suffering like an old yellow wood carving. Her coffee-colored eyes always seemed to have a veil over them, as if she were hiding a terrible secret. She avoided people; swathed in her long black scarf she stole down the street furtively, as if conscious of the eyes of the world.

Her husband was in jail for murder. One summer night (I shall never forget it), he burst from the tenement into the street, screaming like a madman. A revolver was in his hand. We were sitting on the stoop, calmly eating ice-cream cones. The spectacle of this wild swarthy Italian in his undershirt, shrieking, and waving a pistol, appalled us like a hallucination. He rushed by us, and dived into a cellar. A crowd gathered. A policeman ran up. He hadn't the nerve to follow the Italian into the cellar, but stood uncertainly on the sidewalk, growling: "Get up out of there, before I shoot yuh." At last the Italian stumbled out, sobbing like a child. His bronzed, rocky face was grotesquely twisted with grief. He wrung his hands, beat his chest, and clawed at his cheeks until the blood spurted. I have never heard such dreadful animal howls, the ferocious and dangerous agony of a dying wolf. He had just killed his brother in a quarrel over a card game.

This passion-blinded assassin was Betsy's husband. She was left with three children, and no friends. She could speak only Italian. My mother visited her, and through sheer sympathy, learned, in the course of several visits, a kind of pigeon-Italian. It was marvelous to hear my mother hold hour-long conversations with this woman, in a polyglot jargon that was a mixture of Italian, Yiddish, Hungarian and English. But the women understood each other.

My mother helped Betsy find a clothing shop that would give her basting work to do at home. My mother helped the Christian in many ways. And Betsy worshipped her. In the midst of her miseries she found time to knit a large wool shawl as a surprise for my mother. She brought it in one night, and cried and jabbered excitedly in Italian, and kissed my mother's hands. And my mother cried, and kissed her, too. We could not understand a word of what they were saying, but my mother kept repeating in Yiddish: "Ach, what a good woman this is! What a dear woman!" My mother treasured this shawl more than anything she owned. She liked to show it to every one, and tell the story of how Betsy had made it.

A shawl like that was worth over ten dollars, more than Betsy earned in a week. It must have taken weeks to knit, many overtime nights under the gaslight after a weary sixteen-hour day at basting clothing. Such gifts are worthy to be treasured; they are knitted in love.

8

THERE was an Irish family living on the top floor of our tenement. Mr. O'Brien was a truck-driver, a tall gloomy giant with a red face hard as shark-leather. He came home from work at nine and ten o'clock each night. Powerful and hairy in his blue overalls, he stamped ponderously up the stairs. If we children were playing in the halls, he brushed through our games, scowling at us as if he hated children.

"Get the hell out of my way; you're thick as bed-bugs," he muttered, and we scattered from under the feet of the ferocious great Christian.

His wife was also large and red-faced, a soft, sad mountain of flesh waddling around under perpetual baskets of laundry. All Christian ladies did washing, all except the Italians. Mrs. O'Brien was kinder to children than her husband, but we feared her almost as much.

This couple was one of the scandals of the tenement. Night after night, in the restless sleep of our little commune, we heard as in a coöperative nightmare the anguished screams of the Irish mother down the airshaft. Her husband was drunk and was beating her.

"No, no, Jack, don't!" she screamed. "You'll frighten the boy."

This couple had a mysterious child whom nobody had ever seen, and the mother always mentioned him in these brutal midnight scenes.

"Tuh hell with the boy!" roared the man's voice, formidable and deep as a mad bull's. "Tuh hell with everything!"

Crash! he had knocked her down over a table. Windows flew open; heads popped into the airshaft from every side like a shower of curious balloons; the tenement was awake and fascinated. We could hear a child's frightened whimpering, then crash! another powerful blow struck at a soft woman's body.

"Jack, don't! The neighbors will hear!"

"Tuh hell with the kikes! I'll set fire to the damn house and make the sheenies run like rats!"

Bang, crash, scream! The tenement listened with horror. These were the Christians again. No Jew was ever as violent as that. No Jew struck a woman. My mother, ever an agitator, led a campaign against the Irish couple, to force the landlord to put them out. "It is worse than the whores," said my mother, "having Christians in a tenement is worse."

9

BUT one quiet afternoon, who should burst into my mother's kitchen, pale and stammering with fright, but the Irish washerlady.

"Quick, my boy is choking to death! Help me! Get a doctor, for God's sake!"

My mother, without a superfluous word, sped like a fireman up the stairs, to help the child. It had swallowed a fishbone. My mother, expert and brave in such emergencies, put her finger down his throat and dislodged the bone. Then she had a long intimate talk with the Irish mother.

That night at the supper table, while my work-weary father was trying to eat hamburger steak, and read the Yiddish newspaper, and drink beer, and think about his troubles, and smoke and talk all at the same time, my mother irritated him by sighing profoundly.

"Ach, Herman," she said, "that Irish washerlady has so many misfortunes."

"*Pfui!*" my father spat impatiently, "so have I!"

"She is a good woman," said my mother, "even if she is a Christian. Her husband beats her, but she is sorry for him. He is not a bad man. He is only sad."

"*Gottenu!*" my father groaned in disgust with female logic. "I hope he beats you, too!"

"He was a farmer in Ireland," my mother went on dreamily. "He hates the city life here, but they are too poor to move to the country. And their boy has been sick for years. All their money goes for doctors. That's why he drinks and beats her, but her heart bleeds for him."

"Enough!" said my father, clutching his hair. "Enough, or I will go mad!"

My mother saw that he was really angry, so she took the empty soup plates into the kitchen. There she stirred something in a pot, and opened the stove to take out the noodle pudding. She brought this to the table.

"And, Herman," she said pensively, with the steaming pudding in her hands, "that woman used to gather mushrooms in the forest in Ireland. Just the way I gathered them in Hungary."

10

I was playing with the boys. We had been seized with the impulse to draw horses in chalk on the pavement. Then there was a fight, because Joey Cohen had written under his horse, "Nigger loves Leah." He also wrote this on an express wagon, on the stoop steps, and on the bock beer sign standing in front of the saloon. Nigger was about ready to punch Joey on the nose, when Mrs. O'Brien shambled up to us, slow, sad and huge, looming above us with the perpetual basket of laundry on her arm.

"Don't fight, boys," she said kindly in her clear Christian speech. "Will one of you do something for me? I will give any boy a nickel who will go up and play with my little boy. He is sick."

We were dumfounded with fear. We stared at her

and our mouths fell open. Even Nigger was scared.

Mrs. O'Brien looked right at me. "Will you do it?" she pleaded. I blushed, and suddenly ran off as if I had seen a devil. The other boys scattered. Mrs. O'Brien sighed, picked up her heavy basket, and hobbled on her way.

I told my mother that night. What did it mean? Was the Christian washerlady trying to snare me into her home, where she would burn a cross on my face with a hot poker?

"No," said my mother thoughtfully. "Go up there; it will be a good deed. The Christian child is lonely. Nothing can happen to you."

She took me there herself the next morning. And I found nothing to fear. It was a gray humid morning. In the yellow gloom of a bedroom narrow and damp like a coffin, a child with shrunken face lay in bed. His forehead was pale as marble. It was streaked with blue veins, and altogether too round and large for his head. His head was too large for his body. It dangled clumsily, though supported by a steel brace at the neck.

He looked at me with great mournful eyes. His nose wrinkled like a baby's, and he cried.

"Don't be frightened, Johnnie," said his mother, "this boy is a friend who has come to play with you."

I wound my top and spun it on the floor. He craned his stiff neck to watch. Then I put the top in his hand

and tried to teach him to spin it, too. But he was too feeble for this sport. So he wept once more, and I was grieved for him. Was this one of the dreaded Christians?

∞∞∞∞∞∞∞∞∞∞∞∞∞∞∞∞∞∞∞∞∞∞∞∞∞∞∞∞∞∞∞∞∞∞∞∞

CHAPTER 14

BUFFALO BILL
AND THE MESSIAH

1

WHAT a crazy mingling of races and religions on my street. I heard most of the languages when I was a child. Germans, Poles, Russians, Armenians, Irish, Chinese; there were always a few of these aliens living among our Jews. Once my father fetched a Negro to supper. My father beamed with pride.

"Katie, do not be frightened," he said. "This black man is one of us. He is an African Jew. I met him in the synagogue. Imagine, he prays in Hebrew like the rest of us!"

The Negro, tall, stiff, unsmiling, mysterious as death in a black suit of clothes, kissed the *mezzuzah* over our door. Then he salaamed until his forehead almost touched the floor. He greeted my mother solemnly:

"*Sholem Aleichem!* Peace be with you!"

"*Aleichem Sholem!*" my mother answered. "With you, Peace!"

Before sitting down to eat, the Negro stranger

washed his hands piously and muttered a Hebrew
prayer. Before each course that was served he recited
the proper Hebrew blessing. What an ultra-pious Jew.
My mother was thrilled by such orthodoxy in a black
man. She stole out between the soup and the fish to
inform the neighbors. Reb Samuel and others came
in to witness the miracle.

They questioned the stranger after supper. He
proved to be a Tartar. Before the evening was over
he had quarreled with every one. Harshly and firmly,
he insisted that he was a better Jew than any one
present. He was an Abyssinian Jew, descended from
the mating of King Solomon and the Queen of Sheba.
We others had wandered among the Gentiles, he said,
and had been corrupted. But his people had kept the
faith pure. For instance, we prayed only at morning
and evening. His congregation prayed four times a
day. We used seven twists in binding on the phylacteries. His people used nine. And so on, and so on.
He was very dogmatic. He out-talked every one. Reb
Samuel was dumfounded. My father hung his head
in shame. At last the Negro left haughtily, kissing the
mezzuzah again. By his manner one could see he despised us all as backsliders, as mere pretenders to the
proud title of Jew.

2

GYPSIES camped one winter in a vacant store on our
street. Twelve men and women, and some twenty

lusty, filthy children, they added a gala note to the
drab street. I could see their way of living from our
back windows. They had no furniture. They slept on
the floor at night, and ate their meals from newspapers
spread on the floor. They squatted in three circles
while eating. The men sat in the first ring nearest the
food, the women behind them, and then the children.
The gamins roamed around restlessly, and snatched
like dogs at tidbits thrown them. Every one shouted,
fought, laughed while they grabbed meat from the
common bowl.

These gypsies made a lot of trouble on our street.
They visited grocery stores and butchers. While a
gypsy woman talked the most astonishing nonsense to
the proprietor, and held him hypnotized, the others
would steal things. The gypsy men mended pots and
pans for the East Side housewives. The women told
fortunes with cards and read palms. Several visitors
to the gypsy store lost their watches in there; an old
woman lost her purse. Every one got to fear the
gypsies in our midst, yet chuckled and smiled fondly
when they passed in their gay, flaming dresses. Ach,
it was like Europe. It made my mother homesick to
see them. My mother had known gypsies in Hungary,
and could speak a few gypsy words.

Late one night all the kerosene lamps were lit in
the gypsy store. I looked in and saw a party. The
children were crowded against the wall, and a gypsy

woman in a brilliant red shawl danced for them. She
sang as she danced. The children clapped their hands
in time, and called to her.

My mother, like all the mothers along the street,
warned me against the gypsy children. "Don't play
with them; they are filthy with lice." But she herself
had played with gypsies when a child in Hungary;
she told me so herself.

A day came in spring, warm and luring. A closed
wagon drew up before the store. The gypsies piled
into it laughing and chattering, with all their pots,
pans, bedding, filth. They drove off while the crowd
on the sidewalk booed them good-naturedly.

3

WE were near Chinatown. At various times Chinese
lived in our tenement. Once a group of fifteen chop
suey waiters moved into one of the flats. They were
a nuisance from the start. They never seemed to sleep.
All night long one heard a Chinese phonograph whining and banging horribly. The waiters held long
explosive conversations all night. They quarreled,
played cards, cooked queer dishes that filled the
tenement with sweet, nauseating smells. An opium
den, some of the neighbors said. A gambling house,
said others. One morning there was a crash. Then
the police came and found the house in wreckage.
The young Chinese had disappeared. The nude body

of a white girl lay on the floor. She had swallowed
rat-poison.

4

NEGROES, Chinese, Gypsies, Turks, Germans, Irish,
Jews—and there was even an American on our street.

She was Mary Sugar Bum; she came from Boston.
She was an old vagabond woman who sometimes
worked as a scrubwoman in office buildings. But most
of her days were spent in being violently drunk and
disorderly.

Mary slept in an empty stall in the livery stable.
Vassa, the night watchman, was a kind, pock-marked
old Polack with one eye; his other eye had been kicked
out by a funeral horse. He saw to it that Mary always
had clean straw for her stall, and a blanket in winter.

Some of the most sodden bums made love to Mary.
They bought her a five-cent hooker of rotgut whisky
and took her into an alley while she cursed them and
bargained for more whisky. We children watched this
frequent drama.

Every one knew Mary. With bonnet tipped over
her eyes, her gray hair streaming down her shawl, her
skirt tripping her floppy comical old feet, she appeared screaming on our street, prima donna for an
afternoon. There was an audience at once. Heads
popped out of tenement windows, a crowd assembled,
every one laughed.

In a weird voice, shrill as a cat's, Mary sang old

ballads. She pirouetted, holding her skirts out daintily. Sometimes she kicked them high with a chorus girl's squeal, exposing her horrible underthings. Every one laughed. Then she flopped in the mud, and cursed, and could not rise again. She was too drunk. And we children formed a circle, and taunted her, singing gayly:

> *Lazy Mary, will you get up,*
> *Will you get up to-day?*

This infuriated her. She chased us, flopping again and again, like a bird with broken wings. Her face was spotted with mud; her blue eyes blazed; the rose on her bonnet teetered.

"Where's your wedding suit, Mary?" we yelled. "Where's your husband, Mary?"

This made her rave. When Mary was sober, she liked to talk about her first husband, and the elegant "wedding suit" he gave her when she married him at sixteen. This was her life's romance. Every one knew it, even the children. The worst taunt of all was to remind her of it. It made her rave.

In her worst frenzies, she would pull a knife from her bosom, and scream:

"I'll cut the heart out of every goddamned man in the world!" Then five coach drivers had to grab her, and take her into the stable, where they put the American woman to sleep in her stall.

5

THE red Indians once inhabited the East Side; then came the Dutch, the English, the Irish, then the Germans, Italians and Jews. Each group left its deposits, as in geology.

At Second Avenue and 5th Street there remained a German landmark among the Jews. It was a Lutheran church, a brick building with an old-fashioned porch. One summer morning I saw a curious sight there. A crowd had gathered in front of the church, jeering and booing. There were venerable Jews among them with white beards. They were giggling like boys. What amused the crowd was something almost too metaphysical for words.

The owlish little sexton was scrubbing on the porch with soap and water a tall wooden statue of Jesus.

"Jesus is taking a bath!" the crowd jeered. "Their idol is dirty, he needs a bath!"

The elder Jews were especially cynical. "For this stick of wood we were slaughtered in Europe," one graybeard said to another. The crowd grew bigger and more hilarious each minute. At last a policeman arrived, and shooed it away. There might have been some unpleasant explosion—a stoning, a riot. Such riots had been known in the past.

Once a crowd of young Jewish atheists paraded before the synagogues on Yom Kippur. This is a fast day, the most sacred holiday in the year. The atheists ate ham sandwiches, and shouted blasphemous slogans. Six of them were taken to the hospital with severe wounds.

Another time a mob of religious Jews attacked the funeral of a Jewish girl who married an Italian, and had become a convert. She was being buried in the Catholic Church. Led by her distracted father, the crowd tried to capture her body from the profanation. They were beaten off by the police. Religion was a fervent affair on the East Side. Every persecuted race becomes a race of fanatics.

6

MY mother's eldest brother, Max, was very fanatic. When my parents married, this uncle labored for months to persuade my mother to shave her head, and to put on the orthodox wig of married women. My father fought against the notion. He preferred my mother's natural hair. My mother yielded to him, but lost, as a result, her brother's friendship for life.

Yet my mother was quite pious herself. She observed all the minute, irritating details of the Jewish orthodoxy, a ritual that affects one's most trivial acts, and complicates life like a bad neurosis.

My mother read the morning and evening prayers; but my father did not. He did not put on the phylacteries each morning, or go to synagogue on Saturday.

He attended only on the great holy days. He even smoked on the Sabbath, and committed other sins. He was as careless about religion as he was about many other things.

Once a committee came from his synagogue. They sat in derby hats in our front room, and their spokesman solemnly chided my father for not attending the services on Saturdays.

"It is a great sin, brother," said the chairman. "To neglect the Sabbath is a sin."

"I know it," my father agreed cheerfully, "but I think God will forgive me. He knows my reasons. They are good ones."

Then my father told them a story. One day a rich man asked God for a favor. God granted it to him promptly. The next day a poor man asked for something. God refused him as promptly. A young Angel standing near the throne was shocked.

"What, can this be right?" he said to God. "Look, that rich man needs no help but at once you gave him what he asked. The poor man you turned away. God, I ask you frankly, is this justice?"

"Yes," said God, smiling. "That poor man is a perfect pest. Every day he is asking me for something. But the rich man asks me only once in a great while. So, *pfui* on it, let him have it! He won't bother me so soon again."

"So that's what it is, brothers," said my father in

conclusion to the committee. "I am poor and don't want to bother God too often with my prayers. Why should I annoy Him?"

The committee wagged its beards dubiously at this joke, and left our home filled with dark suspicions. Just the same, my father was a loyal Jew. In our home all the Mosaic taboos were observed. There was a *mezzuzah* over the door, and he kissed it before going to work in the morning. He fasted on the Day of Atonement, beat his breast and wept with the congregation. On the two Passover nights he put on a long white robe and presided at the sacred banquets.

7

OLD BARNEY was one of the odd characters on our street. He was a Jew of seventy who worked as porter for a basement factory that made brass beds. Winter and summer he was rigged in a fantastic costume, a cloak green with age and stuffed with rags. There must have been fifteen pounds of the rags, but even in the summer heat he shed none of them. He lugged the heavy bedsteads, sweated terribly, but was faithful to his stinking rags.

There were always curious people watching Barney as he worked, or while he sat resting on the stoop, his long pilgrim's staff in his hand. Some of them whispered that he was a miser, and had money concealed in his rags. Others said he was only crazy. Sure of their own sanity, they argued with him at great length, to prove to him that it wasn't normal to wear fifteen pounds of rags in summer. But Old Barney never argued; he clung to his rags. The brass-voiced drivers tried to make him angry; they flung filthy jokes at him. Barney stared at them with his melancholy eyes, and beat them down with his majestic silence. People laughed at him, yet there was something awe-inspiring in that crazy old man's face, with its quiet patience, suffering, remoteness.

One question made Barney talk. The giggling children would gather around and ask:

"Barney, what are you waiting here for?"

The mad, solemn eyes turned upon us, and the old man said slowly:

"I am waiting for the Messiah, my children."

"And what will the Messiah bring you, Barney?"

"A glass of cream soda," he said.

We laughed and scampered away. The old man was not hurt by our laughter, but sat there waiting. I sometimes asked him other questions, because I believed the Messiah was coming, too. It was the one point in the Jewish religion I could understand clearly. We had no Santa Claus, but we had a Messiah.

8

THE Jewish holidays were fascinating to children It was like having a dozen Christmases during the year.

I liked the Hanukah candle festival, and the joy at
the Jewish New Year. I liked the romantic Succoth
feast, when primitive shacks roofed with bulrushes
were built in the tenement yards, for East Side Jews
to feast in as a memory of their wander-years in the
Arabian desert.

The synagogue services were amusing at times. It
was like a theater. The Rabbi blew a ram's horn, and
a hundred bearded men wrapped in shrouds convulsed
themselves in agony. They groaned, sobbed, beat their
breasts and wailed those strange Oriental melodies,
that are two thousand years old, yet still move the
Jewish heart.

A boy was awed by this passion. But mostly the
congregation droned through hours and hours of
meaningless Hebrew. The synagogue stank with bad
air; the windows were always locked. People gossiped, yawned, belched, took snuff, talked business,
and spat on the floor. Even the grown-ups were bored.
And so a boy wriggled from his father's side, and
rolled dice for picture buttons with other bored young-
sters in the hallway.

My interest in the Messiah began on a summer day.
My gang had gone off to fish for lafayettes at some
river dock, and I had missed them. I was all alone
on my street, and there was nothing to do. I walked
down to the Bowery: here there was always something
exciting.

I lingered around the doors of saloons. I heard men shouting inside, and pianos going. Then I dared to stroll a little further down, to the ten- and twenty-cent lodging houses. Bums in blue cotton shirts lounged around; one of them glared at me and I ran away. I came to the employment agencies. Here I watched the pullers-in at work. They bullied the big laborers in overalls who wandered past. They snatched them out of their aimless dreaming before the signboards and dragged them inside, to be shipped off on some job.

I spelled out the chalk writing on the signboards: 60 Men Wanted for Lumber Camp Upstate; Men Wanted for Section Gangs. I wondered what section gangs were like, and lumber camps. Then I saw two drunken men in overalls punching at each other. One slipped. The other kicked at his face until it was a bloody mash. A cop arrested them. A police wagon clanged its way to the curbing, and they were flung in like logs. A crowd hooted and laughed as they were driven off.

I had two pennies. I decided to go to Chinatown and buy some sugar-cane. This would be a great adventure. I would see if I were brave. I would go there by way of Mulberry Street. That was the land of the heredi-tary enemy—the Italians lived there. I might be killed. But Buffalo Bill would have gone by way of Mulberry Street. I must make myself as brave as

Buffalo Bill. He was my hero then; I was reading the gaudy little paper books that described his adventures.

I walked down Hester Street toward Mulberry. Yes, it was like the Wild West. Under the fierce sky Buffalo Bill and I chased buffalo over the vast plains. We shot them down in hundreds. Then a secret message was sent us from a beautiful white maiden. She was a prisoner in the camp of the Indians. The cruel redskins were about to torture her. Buffalo Bill and I rode and rode and rode. In the nick of time we saved her. Two hundred cruel redskins bit the dust before our trusty rifles. We escaped with the white girl, and rode and rode and rode.

So why should I fear these Italian boys? I saw two of them rolling an iron hoop down the street. My knees shook. I pretended to myself I was a spy and walked along as if I belonged here. I looked around carelessly. I saw the Italian pushcarts. They were heaped with strange green vegetables I had never seen. I saw an old Italian man who wore earrings. I saw Christians eating oysters and clams at a pushcart; I had heard of this, but not believed it. I saw a pig's head on exhibition in a butcher's window; another dirty but fascinating object eaten by Christians.

Bang. I had been slugged over the head. I jumped in surprise and turned to see who had hit me. I was in the hands of the enemy! Eight Italian boys with sticks surrounded me, whooping like Indians. Their eyes gleamed, their faces were cruel. The thing I feared most had happened.

The leader, a big strong boy, clutched my collar, and asked fiercely:

"What streeter?"

I was confused, and made a great tactical blunder. I told the truth.

"Chrystie Street," I said.

"Hooray, a Jew, a Jew!" he screamed, his face lighting up with a boy's joyous cruelty. He slugged me with his stick. The others yelled and joined in the slugging. I fell to the pavement, then fought to my feet and ran. Down Mulberry Street I ran. They pursued me, throwing stones, bricks and vegetables.

"Christ-killer!" some one yelled. All the boys took up the ancient cry. The mob grew; there must have been fifty boys chasing me now. A stone caught me on the temple, and I tasted blood on my lips. A brick cut my right shin. My ribs were bruised by the sticks; my shirt slimy with horse-dung and rotten vegetables. I couldn't breathe; my lungs pricked me like needles.

The grown-ups lined the curbing and watched the chase without much interest. Some of them laughed at the juvenile tragedy. I sobbed and ran. I grew weaker. At last I came to the Bowery, and managed to cross it into my own Jewish land.

The Italians were afraid to follow me across the

Bowery; some of my own gang might attack them here. They remained on their own side, and yelled a last exultant "Christ-killer!" as they watched me trot safely home.

9

I SAT in my mother's lap, sobbing, while she washed away the blood and filth. She scolded me, kissed me, and cursed the bad Christians who had done this.

"Who is Christ, momma?"

"It is their false Messiah!" said my mother, bitterly.

"But I didn't kill him! Why do they say I killed him?"

"Of course you didn't kill him, darling. Don't cry so. The Christians killed him, and now they blame us for it."

"But who was Christ, momma?"

"He was a bad magician who wanted to make the Jews believe he was the Messiah. But we laughed at him, so he hated us, and betrayed his own race to the Gentiles."

"And he really wasn't the Messiah?"

"Of course not. When the Messiah comes he will save the world. He will make everything good. That false Messiah made things only worse. Look at the world; liars and thieves everywhere, wars, murders, and children killed with street cars! When the true Messiah comes he will change all this."

"When will he come, momma?"

"I don't know. Ask Reb Samuel; maybe he can tell you."

The thing pressed on my mind. I asked Reb Samuel in his umbrella store that afternoon. He said the Messiah might not come for many years. He would ride a white horse and put to shame every enemy of the Jews.

Would he look like Buffalo Bill? I asked.

No. He would be pale, young and peaceful. He would not shoot people down, but would conquer them with love.

I was disappointed. I needed a Messiah who would look like Buffalo Bill, and who could annihilate our enemies. I had many talks with Reb Samuel about this.

CHAPTER 15

THE SAINT OF THE UMBRELLA STORE

1

REB SAMUEL hummed Chassidic hymns as he worked at his machine in the umbrella store. He was trying to forget America. But who can do that? It roared in the street outside, it fought against him from the lips of his own children. It even reached into his synagogue, and struck at his God.

It finally defeated him, this America; it broke the old man, because he could not bend.

Tall, frail, austere, there was a dignity about Reb Samuel that made every one respect him. His face, white as Siberian snow, with beard as white, was pure and solemn as a child's. It was transparent as if he never ate. His large blue eyes were calm with spiritual certainties. He had that air of grandeur that surrounds so many old pious Jews. The world can move them no longer; they have seen and suffered all.

Reb Samuel never hurried; he was never angry. He walked through the filth and chaos of our street leaning on his staff, a stately Prince of Zion in exile. Talmudic texts interpolated his ordinary talk. When one of his children cried, he soothed it with quotations

from the great Rabbis. Even as he sat in his miserable
shop, sewing umbrella tops all day, an eternal dignity
rested on him.

He liked to have me come into the store and talk
to him while he worked. My mother's father in Hungary had been a Chassid like Reb Samuel. The old
man would remind me of my tradition, and urge me
to be true to it.

The Chassidim are a sect who revolted some three
hundred years ago against the dry formalism into
which Judaism had sunk. They were mystics whose
exaltation bordered on hysteria. In their synagogues
to-day they still leap, dance, and sing like Holy
Rollers, seeking the *Dveikuss*, the ecstasy in which
man is united with God.

Chassidim look down on other orthodox Jews, and
call them the *"Misnagdem,"* the worldly ones, the
outsiders. And these others sneer in turn at the
Chassidim, and call them madmen and drunkards.

"But we are not drunkards," Reb Samuel would
say quietly. "It is true we use wine and food to show
our joy in God. Food is holy; wine is holy; God is
everywhere, even among these umbrellas that I am
sewing. Do you understand, Mechel?"

"Yes, Reb Samuel."

"You must learn to do good deeds, for every good
deed hastens the coming of the Messiah. You want
Him to look like Buffalo Bill. I tell you, He will not

look like Buffalo Bill, nor will He kill any one. He will come to save the world, not to destroy it, like the false Messiah of the Christians. First He will redeem the Jews, then the other nations. This is why we now must suffer more than the rest of humanity. This is why Chassidim rejoice in the midst of suffering. We Jews have been chosen; we are fortunate. Do you understand what I am teaching you, my child?"

"Yes, Reb Samuel."

"And now repeat after me these words. I believe—"

"I believe," I chanted in the rich Hebrew vowels:

"In the coming of the Messiah—"

"In the coming of the Messiah—"

"And though He tarry, I will wait daily for His coming."

"And though He tarry, I will wait daily for His coming," I chanted in the ancient singsong.

Reb Samuel patted my head gently.

"Good," he said. "You will make a better Jew than my own stubborn children. You have a Jewish heart. To-morrow I will teach you the rest of the Credo."

Reb Samuel was the spiritual leader of a small congregation of Chassidim. Often they would come to his home and talk and sing, and I would sit quietly and listen.

They fascinated me. They were as mysterious as the folk in my father's fairy-tales. They were not pale East Side carpenters, tailors and peddlers, but sorcerers and spirits. They drank tiny glasses of brandy, and then danced in a circle, clapping their hands. Their beards wagged, their eyes were shut in ecstasy, the big veins throbbed in their throats as they wailed the hypnotic desert melodies. It was weird; and something deep inside of me responded to it.

2

At first Reb Samuel had tried to manage the umbrella business. But he had no mind for figures; he believed in every one's honesty; he was above the petty things. The business was being destroyed, and so his wife had to take it over. He went on working at the machine. Reb Samuel was glad of this arrangement. It left his mind free for religion.

But it was hard on little Mrs. Ashkenazi, his wife. She was a tiny, gray woman, weighing not more than ninety pounds, and sapped dry as a herring by work. Her eyelids were inflamed with loss of sleep. She slaved from dawn till midnight, cooking and cleaning at home, then working in the umbrella store. At forty she was wrinkled like a woman of seventy. She was always tired, but was a sweet, kindly, uncomplaining soul, who worshiped her family, and revered her impractical husband.

The shop was a dreary hole. It stank like a sewer of glue, dyes, damp cloth and human bodies. Three girls worked at machines alongside of Reb Samuel, sewing umbrella tops. His oldest child, Rachel, a girl of fifteen, drilled holes into umbrella handles at another machine. His little wife steamed umbrellas onto the ribs at a big copper kettle.

The machines clattered; steam hissed; the girls talked or coughed; peddlers and customers came in and out, arguing, bargaining. It was a bedlam at all times, a place of petty tragedy, petty slavery; just another of those thousand cockroach businesses that are scattered over the East Side, and that have but a single point in their favor; each keeps a family alive.

On rainy days the peddlers crowded in. They took bundles of umbrellas on credit, to be sold at elevated stations and street corners. Reb Samuel's wife had to check the bundles in and out. The peddlers were young semi-vagabond Jews, loud blusterers and liars who thought it clever to cheat her. And so the timid little woman had learned to argue brazenly, to fight back, to be bold in defending her family.

Reb Samuel was calm in the midst of the bedlam. He never interfered with his wife's management. He never worried when a week passed and there was no rain. All this was of the world, and for his wife to worry about; Reb Samuel had more serious cares.

3

His Chassidic congregation had no synagogue to worship in. They met at each other's homes for worship;

on holidays they rented a dance hall or lodge room
for the services. And they had no Rabbi.

"Ach, everything is falling to pieces," Reb Samuel
would sigh. Things were happening such as were never
heard of in Jewry. America was conquering even the
Chassidim. The last fort of God in this country was
falling before the enemy.

Reb Samuel was patient with America. He submitted to it as once he had submitted to the pogrom.
He saw Jews working on the Sabbath, Jews eating
pork, and practicing other abominations. He learned
to shrug his shoulders and be silent.

But a member of his own sect went so far as to
shave his orthodox beard, because in America beards
are laughed at. This was going too far. At this point
the dreamy Reb Samuel made a stand.

He demanded that the criminal be expelled from
the Chassidic congregation. The man, a shrewd dry
goods merchant, rose boldly at the meeting and ad-
vanced the following arguments:

"Brother Chassidim," he said, "I have not broken
the Mosaic law by taking off my beard, and I can
prove it. What says the Law on this point, brothers?
It says plainly: Thou shalt not trim or cut the corners
of thy beard. What does this mean? How does one
trim or cut a beard? With a scissors or razor. Our
holy law-giver Moses had these in mind when he
uttered his commandment.

"But, brothers, do I use a scissors or razor on my beard? No; I use a white powder. In America the wise men have invented a powder that eats away the beard without cutting or shaving. It is this powder that I use. A famous Rabbi in the Bronx uses it. Many pious Jews and Chassidim are using it. It is not forbidden, brothers. I am as good a Chassid as Reb Samuel! May God smite my children if I use razor or scissors!"

This bold, plausible defense made a great impression on the congregation of mystics. Others of them had found the long orthodox beard a handicap in America and were secretly attracted by any legal way out. The dry goods merchant was not expelled. And a week later two other members of the congregation appeared without beards. They, too, were using the depilatory. Reb Samuel's soul was shaken to its core. The fervent, simple old man could not sleep nights for worry.

With other ultra-orthodox factionalists he discussed the matter. They reached the conclusion that a synagogue was needed at once, and a Rabbi—a leader—a general in the war against America. So for the next five years these poor carpenters, umbrella-makers and sweatshop slaves deprived themselves of food, and their children of food, that a permanent synagogue might be leased and a Rabbi brought from Europe—a real Rabbi, not one of these American compromisers.

They fetched over the great-great-great-grandson of a Zaddik who had been famous all through Poland, Lithuania and Russia.

These Zaddiks were reputed to be descended from the thirty-six Wise Men of Israel; the thirty-six who were the last remnant of the Lost Tribes. Unknown, unheralded, in rags and humility, they wandered over the world and appeared at crucial moments when the Jewish nation needed them most.

The famous Zaddik had performed his miracles around the year 1810. Such virtue is considered hereditary, and his descendants had lived in the same region for two hundred years, working the same miracles. Reb Samuel and his congregation brothers learned that the present vessel of the original Zaddik's virtues was anxious to come to America. Times were bad; his congregation was starving; he, too, was living lean.

They sent him a steamship ticket and some money, and waited for him as for the Messiah.

"Ach, when the Rabbi Schmarya comes, how different everything will be!" Reb Samuel would say.

4

AT last the dream came true. It was a summer morning. A strange medieval parade walked down our street. The new Rabbi was being escorted to the new synagogue.

I have seen pictures of religious processions in
India. Theatrical, exotic and fierce with unaccountable
passions, they remind me of that summer parade on
my street. A hundred bearded Jews wrapped like
Bedouins in white praying shawls were marching
slowly. The tenement windows and sidewalks were
lined with spectators. The Chassidim were mad with
holy joy. They skipped like children, they sang, they
clapped their hands, they kissed each other with naked
ecstasy. Reb Samuel led the ecstatic mob of bearded
men. He was pale with emotion, and carried the synagogue Torah in his arms. It was ponderous, this huge
scroll of parchment dressed like a king's child in
precious silk and gold. But it was the Holy Law, and
the old man hugged it tenderly in his arms, and sang
in a high, trembling voice.

At last, at last! Hope had arrived to the East Side.
God was looking down on Chrystie Street! Some of
the older Chassidim wept. They flung themselves
about in grotesque pinwheels, and shouted, and ig-
nored the smiles and jeers of the more cynical on-
lookers. What mattered dignity now? God was to
dwell in America!

In the center of the parade, reposing on the plush
cushions of an open barouche drawn by four white
horses, appeared the descendant of the miracle-
working Zaddik and of the thirty-six Wise Men; the
Rabbi Schmarya himself.

I was disappointed. I had caught some of Reb Samuel's exaltation and had imagined some Rabbi like a shining angel in white, all beautiful with a golden aureole. But I saw a fat, dull-faced man in a frock coat and high hat. He was obviously pleased with the new silk hat, and fiddled with it. His face held no ecstasy but beefy smugness.

He leaned back, blasé as a fat African king. His heavy eyelids blinked, as without emotion he regarded the whores, peddlers, saloon riffraff, graybeards, and tearful Jewish men and women around him. These were his subjects, and one could guess he knew how to rule them. His royal calm was broken only by noisy children who broke through the parade and tried to shake his hand. He pushed the children away, and squeaked ridiculously. He slapped the face of one boy bolder than the rest. The Rabbi did not seem to like children.

I followed the procession into the synagogue on Forsythe Street, in the basement of a tenement. Here I watched, with a child's cruel intelligence, the Rabbi in the midst of his flock.

The Chassidim were still chattering, laughing, kissing each other. Some wept with emotion; a large group formed a circle at one end of the synagogue, and danced a sacred rondo to their own singing. At rhythmic intervals they flung their arms to the ceiling, and uttered a howl of primeval joy and pain: then

danced again, whipping themselves into a state of delirium.

But the new Rabbi was not abandoning himself to the sacred rage. He was busy eating. He had immediately sat down at the refreshment table, and was stuffing himself with herring, sponge-cake, *apfelstrudel*, *gefulte fish*, and raisins. He devoured platters of food until his eyes popped, and sweat covered his face.

I was disturbed by his gorging, not for esthetic or religious reasons, but because I was hoping to eat some of the food myself. With a host of other small boys of Chassidic connection, I was waiting until the ceremonies were over, and the refreshments served. But the Rabbi was definitely eating up all those refreshments.

I found Reb Samuel leaping solemnly with a group of the mystics, and plucked at his *talith*.

"Reb Samuel," I said anxiously, "the new Rabbi is eating up all the food. There will be nothing left!"

Reb Samuel broke off his ecstasy to glare at me. He walked me into a quiet corner, and shook his finger at me, while his face twitched with anger. I had never seen Reb Samuel so angry before.

"Go home!" he said. "You have committed a sin in talking so stupidly about our Rabbi Schmarya. For this I want you to go home!"

"But Reb Samuel," I pleaded, "I didn't mean to say anything bad."

"Go home!" he repeated, and stalked away. I felt mean. I hadn't meant to make Reb Samuel angry; I liked him too well. But I didn't want to go without tasting some of the nuts, raisins, apples and cakes that were heaped so high on the tables. Yet what apologies could I offer to Reb Samuel? Wasn't it true that the Rabbi was eating up all the food?

I lingered at the fringes of the crowd for some minutes. Reb Samuel saw me again. He motioned sternly for me to go. So home I went, furious at the new Rabbi who had cheated me out of food and experience.

5

ALAS for Reb Samuel. He should have been warned by a child's truthful impressions. I was right about the new Rabbi, and he was wrong.

The Rabbi, who had been such a saint and miracle-worker in Europe, changed in the electric air of America.

For one thing, his scale of living went up by leaps and bounds. He made many demands on his little flock. Reb Samuel neglected his umbrella shop entirely, and spent weeks and months raising money to buy the Rabbi a home in Brooklyn. The Rabbi demanded that his wife and children be sent for from

Europe. That took more money-raising. The Rabbi's family needed a servant. More money.

Reb Samuel did not begrudge the Rabbi these luxuries: they were due the great man. What made Reb Samuel paler, gaunter, and melancholy as months passed was that the Rabbi took no firm stand on the heresy of beards. Reb Samuel was too loyal to say it, but other Chassidim whispered that the new Rabbi was friendly to the Depilatory faction. They were the richer group in the synagogue, and he seemed to prefer the rich.

The climax came a year after his arrival. One day the Rabbi deserted his congregation. He had been offered a better-paying job by a wealthy and un-Chassidic congregation in the Bronx. He wrote a brief announcement to his flock, and simply never appeared again.

The blow crushed my teacher, Reb Samuel. He rarely spoke at home, or in the umbrella shop; he brooded within himself. His eyes lost their peace; his face no longer reflected the eternities. He became a tired, bewildered, lonely old Jew.

He returned one night from one of the many bitter meetings at the congregation, where the factions now quarreled endlessly. He opened the door of his home, and stood at the threshold. His face was ghastly with suffering. His wife looked up from the kitchen stove

in amazement. She waited for him to walk into the
room.

But he lingered strangely. Then a look of unspeak-
able surprise passed over his face. His stick clattered
to the ground; he clutched at his heart.

In a strangled voice he exclaimed:

"What's the matter? What's the matter? What's the
matter?"

Before his wife could reach him, he collapsed to
the floor. He tried to talk to her, but his tongue
strangled. Queer, terrible, animal sounds came forth.
He wept and wept as he made the vain effort to com-
municate with her. He could not get up from the
floor. He could not move his arms and legs. Dr.
Axelrod, after examining him, announced that Reb
Samuel was paralyzed and needed a long rest.

6

FOR the next ten years, while I was growing up, Reb
Samuel lay in bed and rested. He could not stir, he
could not speak above a painful whisper. He lived on
crackers and milk and faded to a white, mournful
skeleton.

His little wife arose now an hour earlier each
morning to sponge him, to spoon-feed him like a
child, to fix his bedpan and other needs. Then she
worked in the umbrella store and returned at noon to
care for him again.

He lay by the window. My father arranged three mirrors in such a fashion that everything below reflected into a mirror hung from the ceiling. Without turning his eyes, Reb Samuel could see everything in the street. He was a man at a never-ending play. He was a spectator, a ghost watching our crazy world.

He was still gentle. He would smile and whisper, "Ach, America! Who can understand America?" Every night his wife talked to him about their children, and about the problems of the umbrella store. He gently gave her comfort and advice.

When he died, every one on the street was sad and went to his funeral. *"Ai,"* the people said, shaking their heads, "Reb Samuel was such a good man and so truly pious! Men like this do not grow on every bush in America! He lived by umbrella-making, but in his heart he was a saint!"

~~~~~~

CHAPTER 16

HOW TO BECOME A MILLIONAIRE

1

MY father was in one of his gloomy periods, when he felt like a failure in America, and cursed, moaned, drank, smoked and seethed with ambitions.

"What have I accomplished?" he asked, beating his breast at the supper table. "I am fifteen years in this country, and am still a house painter. But every day Nathan Schiff becomes richer, and Baruch Goldfarb's picture appears in the newspapers."

"So what of it?" my mother spoke sharply. "Eat your soup."

"What is soup?" my father said tragically. "Soup does not satisfy my soul! I am a slave!"

"A black year on this worrying!" my mother cried. "I am sick of it. What do you want? We are not rich, but bread enough we have. A roof over our heads we have. The children are healthy; we are all alive, thank God! What more do you want?"

"I want to be a Boss!" said my father. "A woman does not understand such things."

"Was your Boss angry again to-day?" my mother asked sympathetically.

"Ach, that louse! He buzzed in my ears so much I could crush him!" my father said, as he viciously bit a pickle. "If you could have seen him! Herman, he weeps, you are using too much paint! Herman, you are going to the toilet too often! Herman, you are smoking your pipe too much on my time! What do you want of my life, he weeps, don't you see you are killing an innocent man? *Pfui* on such a Boss!"

"Find another," said my mother placidly. "You have changed bosses before this."

"I don't want a Boss, I tell you!" my father cried. "I want to be my own boss! I am going to see Baruch Goldfarb to-night! Maybe he will lend me three hundred dollars, and I will start my suspender shop again! I must be my own boss or go crazy!"

"You are crazy now," my mother sniffed. "And that Baruch Goldfarb will help you like the last time; he will get you another hole in the head."

"Let us see," said my father.

2

My mother did not like Baruch Goldfarb, or trust him. He was a successful figure on the East Side, a Tammany Hall ward politician, a Zionist leader and the owner of a big dry goods store. He had been a poor boy in the same Roumanian town as my father, and they had emigrated about the same time. For this reason my father felt Baruch was his friend.

Once, as I remember, Baruch came to our home and persuaded my father to vote at the elections.

"It is easy," he told my father. "To-morrow I will make you a citizen, and then the next day you will vote. What could be simpler?"

"It sounds easy," my fascinated father said.

"Of course!" said the great man, slapping him on the back. "All you do is mark a cross under the star. Under the star, remember! You will earn three dollars and be a Democrat. It is a good thing to be a Democrat in America, Herman. It brings one money and friends."

So my father went out to vote. My mother was against the experiment, but who could dissuade my father when he was fascinated? One of Baruch's men took him to vote in three different places. In the third place, a barber shop, a man suddenly hit another man with a blackjack. My father started to leave in great haste, but at the door another man hit my father with a blackjack, too—why, he never could tell.

And so there was a hole in my father's head, and an ambulance had to be called, and he came home wrapped in bandages, disillusioned forever with voting.

"Katie, you were right," he groaned, "voting is only for Irish bums. Never again will I do such a dangerous thing."

But Baruch Goldfarb called again, and had a glib

explanation for what he termed "the accident." My father went on trusting him, but my mother did not.

3

I ACCOMPANIED my father on his visit to Baruch Goldfarb that night. The great man welcomed us warmly into his office back of the dry goods store.

"What a fine boy you have!" he said. "Here is a nickel for ice cream, young man. And here's a good cigar for you, Herman. What's on your mind?"

My father went directly to the point and poured out the history of his life, his suspender shop, his house painting sorrows, his desires to be a boss. Would Baruch lend him three hundred dollars?

Baruch did not answer at first. His massive red face darkened with shadows of important thought. At last, flicking cigar ashes into the cuspidor, he said:

"I will do it! I will raise this money for you, Herman! Not this week, maybe, or next week, but soon. Things are tight for me just now—I have bills to pay. Weren't we boys together in Roumania? Didn't we steal plums and apples from the orchards, and swim in the Danube side by side? Such things one never forgets. I will help you, my friend!"

Then Baruch persuaded my delighted father to join a lodge he had just organized. It was called the "Baruch Goldfarb Benevolent, Sickness, Social and Burial Society." The dues were only ten dollars a year, and assessments, Baruch explained. The benefits were many.

When a member was sick, he received eight dollars a week, and a committee of lodge brothers visited him, wearing their sashes. When he died, he was escorted by, not a mere committee, but the whole membership in sashes, and interred in a reserved plot in the lodge's cemetery. Each member was assured a fine funeral and one of these choice plots. The widow was to receive five hundred dollars made up in assessments.

The lodge would hold dances and vote Democratic at all the city elections. Best of all, the members were solemnly pledged to help each other in a business way.

My father, of course, joined. How could he have resisted such a valuable place in the sun? A few weeks later he took us for a Sunday visit to the cemetery. He proudly showed my mother the burial plot that had been assigned him. He tried to persuade her to join the Women's Auxiliary of the Lodge, and thus reserve a plot next to his.

"Well," said my mother slowly, "I want to be buried beside you, Herman. It is a fine cemetery, too. But first let's see whether that Baruch Goldfarb helps you in business. If he does, I will believe in him, and join the lodge."

My father had no such hesitations and doubts. Baruch Goldfarb became his idol, and the lodge his glorious obsession. My father loved the ritual of the lodge meetings, the secret passwords, the gold and purple sashes and white gloves, the theatrical ceremonies. House painting was drab, but at night life became a wonderful lodge meeting. After the innumerable sessions, he went to the Second Avenue coffee houses with Baruch and the more important officials. How this flattered him.

"They are big men!" he would say jubilantly to my mother. "They are all in business for themselves. It is good to mix with such people; one learns how to make money. And how much they know! Do you know what an Alderman is, Katie?"

"No, and I don't care."

"You ought to care! It is politics! To-night they taught me what an Alderman is, and what is his salary. Another thing they explained to me! Only a person born in America can be President. I cannot be the President, Katie, but our little Mikey can. Think of it!"

"I am thinking," said my mother.

"That Baruch!" my excited father went on, "not only is he a businessman, and our lodge President! He is also secretary of a Zionist club and trustee of a synagogue! It helps him in politics, he says. One must believe in God, he says. The Jews have no country, he says. There will be a boom in Brownsville real estate,

he says. That Baruch, he is also a *real estatnik!* He
says he will sell me a good lot!"

"A luck has bemerded us!" my mother sneered.
"First, tell me, has Baruch done anything to help you
get a shop?"

"Not yet," said my father cheerfully, "but every
day he is thinking it over, he says."

Baruch Goldfarb never did help my father. He
made grand promises, and as grandly forgot them.
But other things happened to my father.

4

My father met a Boss painter at the lodge, Zechariah
Cohen by name. This man took a liking to him.

He hired my father as one of his painters. Because
he was a lodge brother, he asked my father to keep
an eye on the other workers, and secretly report if
they were loafing. My father entered this spy work
with much gusto.

"Zechariah trusts me," he would boast. "Soon he
will fire that Abe Tuchman, and I will have the foreman job. Think of it, Katie, I am on the road to success. Everything is possible in America!"

Tuchman the foreman was a short, bald-headed
man about forty, feeble and sluggish with the same
painter's sickness from which my father suffered. He
had worked for Zechariah for more than ten years.

"He is too friendly with the men, Zechariah says,"

chuckled my father. "On such a foreman a Boss loses money, Zechariah says. And he is slow and always sick. It is certain I will soon be the foreman."

One pay night my father burst into the kitchen, and kissed my mother in a glow of triumph.

"At last I am a foreman!" he cried. "Zechariah made me the foreman to-day!"

"I'm glad," said my mother. She stared at him thoughtfully. "Was that poor man fired?"

"What poor man? Have you discovered some more people to help?"

"You know who I mean," said my mother. "That Abe Tuchman."

"Of course he's fired," said my father impatiently. "He was too slow."

My mother turned away from him.

"What's the matter?" my father asked.

"I will tell you," said my mother. "It is not right that after working ten years for a boss, a man should be fired, a sick man with a family."

"Woman," my father stormed, "attend to your cooking! You are only a woman!"

"Yes," said my mother, and never mentioned the matter again.

5

NEVER did any one put such passion into a foreman's job as did my enthusiastic father in the months that followed.

He no longer dreamed of a suspender shop. He no longer had days of melancholy, when he called himself "the man in a trap." He leaped out of bed in the morning, dashed himself with cold water, and went off whistling to work. He had an air of tremendous hurry. There was no time in the evening to tell us his Roumanian romances; he was too busy with great plans.

My mother did not share his joy. He accused her of being a coward, a pessimist; she only shrugged her shoulders. She was really frightened whenever he became so ambitious. My mother had that dark proletarian instinct which distrusts all that is connected with money-making.

My father was more child-like. He strutted, he declaimed, he was proud of his wonderful new toys. Aha, he was on the road to American success! He had found the secret key of Nathan Schiff and Otto Kahn! No one ever built such glittering lofty castles upon such slight foundations as my father. I am sure now he was meant to be an actor. He smoked many cigars, he drank wine, he wore his black lawyer's suit every evening after work.

He had forgotten Baruch Goldfarb; now he worshiped that splendid, intelligent figure Zechariah Cohen, greatest of all Boss Painters. My father repeated his Boss's jokes; he told us of the stratagems, and remarkable business deals of the Boss; he forced us all to admire his Boss.

6

EVERY ten years there has been a new population on the East Side. As fast as a generation makes some money, it moves to a better section of the city. At that time, the Jews with a little money were moving to the Bronx and to parts of Brooklyn. There was a great land boom in those places; and Zechariah Cohen, like every other money-maker, was dabbling in real estate. His interests lay in a section of Brooklyn named Borough Park.

"We are going to move from the East Side," my father announced one night. "My Boss advised me to move out to Borough Park, where he himself lives. He is willing to sell me a house and lot on the installment plan. He says a man with a future should not live on the East Side."

"But all my friends live here," my mother said. "I would miss them. It is only people with money who live in Borough Park."

"What of it?" said my father. "I also will soon be rich."

7

ONE Sunday we traveled to Borough Park to see the house and lot Zechariah was persuading my father to buy.

It was a dreary day of fall. The suburb was a place of half-finished skeleton houses and piles of lumber

and brick. Paved streets ran in rows between empty
fields where only the weeds rattled. Real estate signs
were stuck everywhere. In the midst of some rusty
cans and muck would be a sign shouting "This Wonderful Apartment House Site for Sale!" In a muddy
pool where ducks paddled, another sign read: "Why
Pay Rent? Build Your House in God's Country."

We walked through a mile of this, and came to a
little dismal settlement, where there were a few shops.
My mother was gloomy, but my father babbled and
orated cheerfully.

"Isn't it a good place?" he asked. "In ten years
every one who now buys here will be rich, Zechariah
says."

We came at last to Zechariah's. It was a large green
house bulging with bay windows and pretentious
cupolas. My father rang the bell, and we waited on
the porch. Zechariah opened the door, and greeted us
cordially. He was a stunted, thickset man puffing
around on short legs like an asthmatic bulldog. He
had shrewd little Mongolian eyes, and a thin nose
spotted like a cheese by smallpox.

"Welcome!" he cried, pumping my father's hand.
"So you have come, Herman!"

"Yes," my father said, flushing with pride at this
cordial reception. "Here are my wife and children."

The Boss patted our heads tolerantly.

"They are nice fat children," he said. "Come in,

don't be bashful. It doesn't cost any money, you know!"

As we entered, there whined from within a petulant female voice.

"Have they wiped their feet, Zechariah? See that they wipe their feet."

The Boss took a worried glance at our shoes. "My wife is strict as the devil," he whispered. "Yes," he added in a loud, cheerful tone, "they have wiped their feet, Sarah. My foreman's family are as clean as we are, hey, Herman?"

He nudged my father slyly, and my father beamed at the familiarity. We came into a large gaudy room glowing with red wallpaper, and stuffed like the show window of a furniture store with tables, chairs, sofas, dressers, bric-a-brac.

8

Mrs. Cohen, a fat, middle-aged woman, lay on a sofa. She glittered like an ice-cream parlor. Her tubby legs rested on a red pillow. Her bleached yellow head blazed with diamond combs and rested on a pillow of green.

She wore a purple silk waist, hung with yards of tapestry and lace. Diamonds shone from her ears; diamond rings sparkled from every finger. She looked like some vulgar, pretentious prostitute, but was only the typical wife of a Jewish *nouveau riche*.

A towel was tied around her forehead, and there was a grieved look on her comical flabby face. She stared at us with open hostility.

"My wife has a headache," Zechariah explained, "so I won't be able to ask you to stay."

"They can stay," the woman sighed, "only the children must not make noise, as the doctor says I am of a very nervous nature."

My father sprang up eagerly. "What, we should annoy you?" he cried. "No, Mrs. Cohen, we will leave at once. We came only to see the house I will buy from Zechariah."

"Nonsense, you must stay!" said Zechariah in a hearty voice. "First we will drink a little brandy; then I will show you the rooms in my house, and *then* we will go to see your own house; ha, ha! Yes, I want you to see my fine expensive furniture, my hand-painted oil paintings, my up-to-date water closet; everything! When you are rich like me, Herman, you will have these things, too!"

They tossed off some brandy; then my father followed the Boss on the sightseeing tour. We were left behind with the Boss's wife. She pressed the towel on her forehead, and sighing like a martyr, said:

"Ach, what a headache! How I have to suffer with these headaches! The doctor says it is because I eat too much, but I only eat as much as my friends. But maybe it's because last night I ate a big ten-course

dinner at Lorber's that cost three-fifty. I should not eat
in restaurants. My cook's food is better for me; I am
of a very nervous nature. She is a good cook; a wonderful cook; we pay her eighty dollars a month, and
our grocery and butcher bill is almost one hundred and
fifty a month. In a good house one should have
only a good cook. This house cost my husband twenty
thousand dollars to build; it is the most expensive
house in Borough Park. What did you pay for your
waist?"

"Two dollars," my mother stammered.

"*Pfui*, I thought so!" said the aristocrat. "For so
little money one can buy only rags. My waists never
cost me less than thirty or forty dollars; and my shoes
twelve dollars; and my hats from fifty dollars up. One
must dress well in our position. And as I often tell my
husband, in the long run it pays to buy only the best.
Don't you think so?"

"Yes," said my mother timidly.

My father returned. He was loud in his admiration
of Zechariah's possessions. The men drank another
brandy, then all of us left Mrs. Cohen on her martyr's
sofa, alone with her headache and her dull, dollar-sign
fantasies.

9

WE walked through slushy weeds under the damp sky.
We came after twenty minutes to a block containing
eight wooden houses, each an exact copy of its ugly

neighbor. Zechariah rubbed his hands with satisfaction, and said proudly:

"Here is it! Look, Herman, the best piece of property in Brooklyn! In five years it will be worth double the price! It is because you are my foreman, and I want to make a man out of you, that I am giving you this chance. All the refined Jewish businessmen are moving here. Irving Shineman has bought one of these houses. He owns that big haberdashery on Rivington Street. There are others like him coming here, too."

He unlocked the front door of one of the homes, and showed my father in. My mother would not go in. She remained on the porch like a beggar. With troubled eyes she stared around her at the suburb, at the lots covered with slush and weeds, at the eight banal houses.

I followed my father into the new house, with its bleak smell of varnish and wood shavings. I heard my father's Boss chant:

"Hardwood floors, Herman! A first class kitchen range free! Electric lights! A modern water closet! *Oy*, what a water closet! Only America has such water closets! Did you ever see in all Europe such a water closet?"

My father was fully as exuberant as the Boss, and I heard him ask the terms.

"It will be easy," said the Boss. "I will take half of your pay for the next four months, and that will pay the first cost, which is three hundred dollars. Then after that I will only take ten dollars a week from your pay. In nine years you will own the house. I have figured it all out for you, Herman."

My father thanked him gratefully.

On our way home, my father asked my mother: "Well, what do you think of it now, Katie?"

"I don't like it," said my mother.

"And why not?" my father said indignantly. "Are you so much in love with that sewer of an East Side?"

"No," said my mother. "But I will be lonesome here. I am used only to plain people; I will miss the neighbors on Chrystie Street."

"But there will be neighbors here," said my father.

"Herman, don't make me do it," my mother pleaded. "I can't do it, Herman. My heart is heavy thinking about it."

"Foolishness!" my father exclaimed, biting his cigar. "We will move here, I say! You must not hold me down! I refuse to be an East Side beggar all my life! Do you hear?"

My mother turned her face from him, and stared at the weeds, the slush, the exultant signboards of Borough Park.

10

It was a Friday evening two months later. Covering her hair with a kerchief, my mother lit the Sabbath candles, and was blessing them. Our home was clean and orderly. It was filled with the quiet domestic sanctities of the Sabbath, which the Jews welcome as a Bride. Supper was hot on the kitchen stove. We children were hungry. My father hadn't come home from work. He was late for a Friday night.

My mother placed the candles on the table. She set the plates, then sat down to wait. A knock sounded at the door. My mother said, "Come in." A haggard little bearded Jew in painter's overalls entered. He looked at my mother forlornly.

"Good Sabbath to you," he stammered.

"Good Sabbath," said my mother, her face pale with premonition.

"I am one of your husband's painters," the man said, licking his dry lips.

"Has something happened?" my mother asked, twisting her apron nervously.

"He has been hurt," said the little painter.

"Hurt?" she gasped.

"He and two others fell into the street. A scaffold broke. Here are his overalls and shirt. He is in Mount Zion hospital. They sent me to tell you."

"He is dead!" my mother wailed.

"No, no, God forbid, not that!" the man reassured her. "He will live, the doctor said. Only his feet are broken, that's all."

My mother sat down in a chair, and in a faint

voice said: "Bring me some water." The man hurried to the sink and brought her a glass of water. She drank it, then began to sob quietly, wiping the tears with the end of her apron.

"My poor Herman! My poor Herman!"

The little house painter tried to comfort her. He wiped his perspiring face with a blue bandanna, blew his nose, and said:

"What's to be done? This happens to all painters; I may be the next to fall; and I, too, have a wife and children. This is the world; we must take what it gives us."

He sent me for the neighbors. When they came, he left, still offering his awkward words of comfort. The neighbors stayed with my mother all night.

My father was brought from the hospital in a month. Both his legs were packed in a block of plaster casting. In falling, he had landed squarely on his feet. Every bone in them was splintered.

He lay in bed for over a year. For three months the Baruch Goldfarb Lodge paid my mother the sick benefit of eight dollars a week. When this income ceased, things became difficult. Zechariah Cohen paid us a visit, then forgot us. Baruch Goldfarb visited us once and forgot us. There was no place we could turn. The payments on the Borough Park house were lost, forever. Lost, too, were my father's dreams of success.

My mother went to work in a Broadway cafeteria.

I took to peddling newspapers after school along the Bowery. Overnight I became a man; I discussed the family finances with my mother; I worried over poverty.

CHAPTER 17

TWO DOCTORS

1

THERE were two doctors on our street, the sad young Dr. Isidore Solow, and the plump, cheerful, middle-aged Dr. Marcus J. Axelrod. Both were kept busy, that winter. There was a fat harvest that year for doctors, druggists, undertakers and charity workers.

The East Side has always been a generous garden for professional people. Many careers of splendor and importance have been founded on this misery of a million Jews.

Poverty in winter. Who can describe, or even imagine, the collective suffering of a hundred thousand tenements? Thousands of tuberculars and paralytics; a vast anemia and hunger; a world of feebleness and of stomachs, livers, and lungs rotting away. Babies groaning and dying in thousands: insomnia—worry.

Pneumonia, Typhoid, and Influenza ran up and down the icy tenement halls, playing deadly tricks like schoolboys on a lark.

There was screaming, hysteria, nervous disease. The funeral coaches rolled through the streets as frequently as the garbage wagons.

225

Dr. Solow grew thinner that winter. His pants flapped from his shrinking hips; his eyes were sunk for want of sleep. But Dr. Marcus J. Axelrod remained cheerful and fat; he blossomed like a rose.

2

IN the old country the Jews worshiped their Rabbis. In this country the Doctor was a community idol. I have seen women follow a young East Side doctor on the street, kiss his hand humbly, sob, and loudly call down God's blessings on his head, as though he were a Savior.

In every pauper Jewish family the mother's dream was to have one of her sons a Doctor, as in every Irish family she dreamed of a Priest.

Dr. Marcus J. Axelrod fulfilled all the Jewish concepts of a doctor. He was pot-bellied and authoritative, with bushy formidable eyebrows and spectacles. His moon face was solemn: from his chin there swung a fine, full, sacred goatee.

While we still had money he was called to attend my sick father. I remember a dark December day. Dr. Axelrod entered like a King into his kingdom. He took off his derby hat, placed his black bag on the floor, and sat by my father's bedside. He stared at my father, then harshly commanded him to show his tongue, and say, "Ah."

Then Dr. Axelrod stroked his goatee grandly. He

called for hot water and a towel. He washed his fat white hands in silence. He stalked up and down, the hands clasped behind his back. He mumbled, he wrinkled his forehead. We watched him reverently. We waited.

At last the great man came out of his travail. He sat down at the kitchen table, blew his nose, and caressed his valuable goatee.

"Bring me a pen and ink," he commanded.

It was brought him. He wrote a prescription. It was as usual for some red, green or yellow medicine; highly colored, and bitter as death. Dr. Axelrod knew his audience; no East Sider respected medicine that did not nauseate.

"He has given me a good strong medicine this time," my father said with satisfaction, as he forced himself to swallow one of these soul-retching compounds.

On some visits Dr. Axelrod asked my mother to give him tea. In every other home the Doctor rushed away after finishing his professional visit. But with us he unbent, and grew familiar. It was because my father and Dr. Axelrod had gone to school together as boys in Roumania.

"Yes," the Doctor grunted, "I well remember the time when we went to school together, Herman. But admit that you had no sense."

"That's right," my father grinned. "I was always a hotheaded young fool."

"Worse," cried the Doctor, "you were a jackass! You might have become a doctor, too, but now see what you are."

"That's right, Herr Doctor," said my father, biting his mustache and sighing.

The Doctor stirred my mother's quince jam and almonds into his tea, and loudly sucked at the spoon.

"Even as a boy," he said, "I knew what the world was like. But Herman didn't. He refused to kiss the priest's hand."

"That's what it was," mumbled my father, "I wouldn't kiss his hand."

"It was a mean priest, a Jew-hater," the Doctor went on. "He came to our schoolroom every morning, and talked on religion. Then we boys had to walk before him and kiss his hand. It was the law; every one had to do it, even the Jews. But one morning Herman refused to do it. Why?"

"I don't know," said my father.

"Because you were a mule," said the Doctor severely. "All the other Jewish boys did it. We had to. Your own father wanted you to do it. But you wouldn't. So you were thrown out of the school. Why were you so obstinate, Herman?"

"I don't know," said my father. "I just couldn't do it any more."

"And this is the price you have paid!" said the Doctor triumphantly, waving his arm about the room.

"You are a sick house painter out of a job. Your wife works in a restaurant, and your children haven't enough to eat. I told you you'd be sorry."

"Yes, Herr Doctor, now I'm sorry," said my father, "but when I was young I had a devil in me."

He grew mournful. The Doctor saw this, and talked of more cheerful subjects. He reminded my father of the happy days the boys went swimming in the Danube, and how they stole plums and apples out of orchards.

"We had some good times, didn't we, Herman?"

"Yes, Herr Doctor," said my father humbly.

3

My father did not seem to get well. His broken feet had healed, and he could hobble around on them. But his stomach, nerves and lungs were still bad because of the paint-sickness. Dr. Axelrod's bitter medicine did not help.

One morning my father leaped out of bed, and said to my mother:

"To hell with being sick! I am tired of it! This morning I will look for a job. A black year on it, things can't go on in this way!"

My mother tried to persuade him to wait a while. He refused angrily. He hunted for a job that day, and the next. On the third day he found a job. My father was happy when he set off to work with his overalls the next morning. He crawled home at noon, however. When my mother came from the restaurant she found him lying in bed.

He began to sob and wring his hands when he saw her.

"Katie," he said, "I can't work any more! I am a ruined man! I will kill myself!"

My mother ran to him and took his hand.

"Hush," said my mother soothing him. "Tell me what has happened."

"I went out on the scaffold," my father sobbed. "I began to work. All was well until I looked down in the street. Then I lost my courage, Katie. My knees shook, and I thought I was about to fall again. The other painter saw that I was sick, but I tried to hide it from him. I went on working. Suddenly I fainted, Katie. He saved me just in time."

"Herman, don't weep so hard," begged my mother. But he was not to be comforted.

"I can never work on a scaffold again," he said. "I have lost my courage for it. Oh, my God, what shall I do now? I have no trade, no money, no courage left! I will kill myself, Katie! I have become a burden!"

"*Shah, shah!*" my mother said gently. "Be patient."

"Where can I borrow three hundred dollars?" said my father wildly. "Oh, if I had three hundred dollars I could start my shop again. I would get out of this miserable housepainting! But I am a man in a trap."

"*Shah*," repeated my mother, "don't worry, Herman. Here, let us drink tea together. It will ease our hearts."

4

DR. AXELROD was called again, but could do nothing. "It is a fright," he said sagely. "Herman has been frightened." He prescribed a strong, bitter medicine. It did not help.

The Doctor frowned when my mother could not pay him for his visit. A second time my mother confessed she could not pay. He went off in a huff. He did not like to call on patients who had no money. This he told my mother frankly on his third and last unpaid visit. He delivered a pompous lecture.

"Should a Doctor starve?" he asked, waving his pudgy hands. "Would it not be a disgrace? I, for one, think so. God knows it is hard enough for a Doctor to make money. He has only his two hands to work with. It is not like being a businessman, with a factory where one hires fifty other hands. I *must* be paid for every visit, my friends. I refuse to starve."

Dr. Axelrod did not call again. Dr. Solow became our family Doctor. No one trusted Dr. Solow: he was too young, he had no beard, he talked plainly and familiarly to people, without any of the grandeur which we expected in a Doctor. But he did not insist on money. That's why he had as many patients as the pompous Dr. Axelrod.

5

DR. ISIDORE SOLOW was a shabby sad young bachelor. No women told him how to dress, so his shirts were always dirty. His hat was a small humorous felt, his black wrinkled suit flapped from his skeleton like a clown's domino.

He was tall and stoop-shouldered. He stared into people's faces absent-mindedly until they were uncomfortable. His eyes were set in deep melancholy hollows. He was gaunt and pale of face like a tragic actor of the old school.

He was eccentric. He popped in and out of places like a ghost, forgetting his umbrella, his medical case, his hat, his watch. Once he even forgot his shoes. It was a confinement case on a hot summer night. He had taken off his shoes while waiting for the labor pains. When the excitement was over he rushed away without the shoes.

He was impulsive, and would blurt out whatever he had in his mind. He told the people they were fools because they slept with closed windows at night. They were horrified. No one ever slept with open windows, they said. It was dangerous. "What, open the windows when there is an iron frost outside?" they exclaimed. "Of course," said Dr. Solow impatiently, "it will save you doctor's bills. But I see you are fools, and want to be sick. Have it your own way."

Once he told a coughing sick man the strangest thing.

"Brother, no medicine can cure you. You must join a labor union."

"A labor union?"

"Yes, a labor union. You slave too many hours in your lousy sweatshop; you get too little pay; you need food and rest, brother. That's what's wrong with you! Join a labor union."

After we came to know him, we loved this young Doctor. He was often in our kitchen, drinking tea. He brought candy and toys for us children. He praised my mother, and said she reminded him of his own dear mother, who was dead.

He was tearful when he talked of his mother.

"Ach!" he sighed, clasping his hands, "what a saint she was! She thought only of me. For ten years she lived in a damp basement on bread and tea. She peddled eggs from a pushcart, and struggled that I might become a Doctor. It was terrible. How often I grew sick of it all, and wanted to throw it up. Such sacrifices seemed to me useless. What is it to be a Doctor, anyway? Is it worth one's mother's life? But she made me go on. Ach, these Jewish mothers! They slave, they suffer, they never give up hoping. So I became a Doctor. And then she died. It is five years now. Ach, my poor little mother, was it worth while?"

"Of course it was worth while," said my own

mother stoutly. "In her grave she is proud of her doctor son."

"Yes," said Dr. Solow sadly, "I know she is. That is the worst part of it all. But I am not proud of being a Doctor. I would like to give it up even now. It hurts me too much. The East Side is too big for a Doctor to cure. I feel too helpless."

"Your heart is too soft," said my mother.

"I know it," said the Doctor. "But what can I do? I would really like to be a farmer. There should be more Jewish farmers in the world."

My father was shocked at this. He broke out:

"What? A Doctor work with his hands like a Roumanian peasant? Permit me to say, Dr. Solow, that such ideas are almost atheistic. What you need is to get married and have children. And you should also raise a beard; that would help you make money like Dr. Axelrod."

"A beard, a wife, money!" the young Doctor sighed, humorously, as he threw up his hands. "My friends, when the East River flows with milk and honey, and not with grease and garbage, then will I have a beard, a wife and money."

My parents found it difficult to understand this Doctor who had so little pride in himself. They needed to worship doctors.

6

IT was that winter that my Aunt Lena appeared with
a satchel one night. She was pale and tired, and sank
into a chair.

"I'm on a strike, Katie," she said. "Can I stay with
you?"

"Of course," said my mother, "things are bad with
us, but you can always stay."

"It will give me a bed anyway," said my aunt.

She gobbled the food my mother set before her at
supper. My mother watched, and said reproachfully:

"You've been going hungry, Lena."

My aunt shrugged her shoulders.

"*Nu*, why not?" she said. "Most of us are going
hungry. That's what a strike means. But the union
is worth it."

My father, that upright conservative pauper, leaped
into action at once.

"A union?" he cried. "I spit on a union! I do not
believe in such nonsense! In America each man should
make his own fortune!"

"Have you made yours?" my aunt asked quietly.

"No," my father exploded, banging with his fork.
"Not yet! All I need is three hundred dollars and I will
start my suspender shop again. You will see, Lena!"

"*Nu*, let us see," my aunt murmured.

"So let us imagine," my father went on fiercely

"that I have found the three hundred dollars and have started my shop. All right! So let us imagine then that I go on working hard in my shop for ten years and have made my fortune. All right! So let us imagine, then, one of your union loafers, a Socialist bum, a freethinker, comes to me and says, Mr. Gold, you are a rich man; give me half your fortune. So what then? Do you think I should give it to him?"

"No," my aunt smiled, "you should keep it. Why should millionaires starve? You have some rights, too."

"Certainly," said my indignant pauper father. Then he realized that my aunt was joking with him. So he sulked during the rest of the meal. But the next night a ferocious argument broke out between the two, that continued every night while my aunt lived with us.

How boldly and vehemently she answered my father. She was no longer the shy, ecstatic little immigrant girl. The sweatshops had hardened her. Her face had lost its naïve beauty. The skin was yellowish with bad health, coarsened and tight over the cheek bones.

She was thinner, she had wrinkles. The sweatshops aged people prematurely. But her mind had grown in the struggle. She amazed us all by her eloquence, by her proud courage and dignity. And her eyes were still beautiful.

My aunt woke at five each morning, and left with-

out breakfast. She had to go on the picket line, she
said. She was busy with the strike all day, and far
into the night. She never got more than four or five
hours sleep. One night she came home with a bandage
around her head. Two Italian gangsters and an Irish
policeman hired by the Jewish bosses had attacked her.

"But how we scratched their faces," she chuckled
grimly. "They will remember us girls."

My mother was horrified. She begged my aunt not
to go into the fire again. But my aunt smiled. "It's
war," she said, and went every morning as usual.

7

How many nights life became glorious because Dr.
Solow entered just at supper time, with arms full of
bundles.

He told us to open them, and behold, we found
spiced beef, and pickles, and salami, and cheesecake,
and other fine things. And we had a feast.

In his own erratic way, Dr. Solow fell in love with
my Aunt Lena. He wanted to marry her. None of us
knew this, not even my aunt, until one night at supper.

Dr. Solow was eating with us. We had come to the
tea-drinking, when suddenly he stopped talking and
stared at my aunt.

He stared at her a long time. It made her uneasy,
but she pretended not to notice. The rest of us did not

disturb him. He was only being absent-minded again, we knew.

My father was in the midst of a sentence, when Dr. Solow came out of his haze as abruptly as he had fallen into it.

"Lena," he said, reaching for my aunt's hand across the table, "I want you to marry me."

My aunt was amazed by this sudden attack. So were the rest of us.

"What?" my aunt repeated, "marry you?" She withdrew her hand.

"Yes," said the Doctor calmly, "it's ridiculous that I should be a bachelor any longer. You, Lena, are the first woman I've met that I think I love."

My father and mother beamed with satisfaction. But my aunt blushed, and stammered painfully:

"No."

"Why not?" the Doctor persisted, staring at her with his absent-minded, penetrating eyes. "Don't you like me, Lena?"

"Of course I do," my aunt said slowly. "You are a good man. Every one likes and respects you. But I can't marry you."

"But give me a reason," the Doctor persisted.

"I can't marry you," my aunt repeated.

My father drank tea out of his saucer with a loud gurgle of disgust.

"Why does she need to give a reason?" he asked

sarcastically. "She is a king's daughter, you know, and every week hundreds of doctors, lawyers, professors and millionaires propose marriage to her, and she refuses them."

"Hush," said my mother.

My aunt rose from the table. There were tears in her eyes.

"Must I tell every one?" she stammered.

Dr. Solow suddenly leaped to his feet.

"No, of course not!" he cried. "Ach, I'm a fool, a fool! I am realizing what a clumsy fool I am, Lena! Proposing to you at the supper table! Ach, my absent-mindedness again! Forgive me, Lena!"

And then the Doctor beat his forehead with his two fists, and clapping on his hat, started to leave the room.

"I'm such a damn fool about everything!" he said.

My Aunt Lena brought him back.

"Sit down," she said, affectionately. "Don't be ashamed, Dr. Solow; you are only too honest. I will tell you my reasons for not marrying you. There is nothing to hide. I am in love with another man. He is one of the strike leaders; he is in jail now."

"Hurrah for the unions! Down with the sweatshops!" the Doctor suddenly shouted.

And then he made us a speech. He forgot that he was in love. My father sulked at first, then grew animated. He defended the rights of millionaires against the enthusiastic Doctor. My mother, my aunt, Mendel the Bum, some of the neighbors drifted in, and even I joined in the orgy of talk that lasted until three in the morning.

CHAPTER 18

THE SOUL OF A LANDLORD

1

ON the East Side people buy their groceries a pinch at a time; three cents' worth of sugar, five cents' worth of butter, everything in penny fractions. The good Jewish black bread that smells of harvest-time, is sliced into a dozen parts and sold for pennies. But that winter even pennies were scarce.

There was a panic on Wall Street. Multitudes were without work; there were strikes, suicides, and food riots. The prostitutes roamed our street like wolves; never was there so much competition among them.

Life froze. The sun vanished from the deathly gray sky. The streets reeked with snow and slush. There were hundreds of evictions. I walked down a street between dripping tenement walls. The rotten slush ate through my shoes. The wind beat on my face. I saw a stack of furniture before a tenement: tables, chairs, a washtub packed with crockery and bed-clothes, a broom, a dresser, a lamp.

The snow covered them. The snow fell, too, on a little Jew and his wife and three children. They huddled in a mournful group by their possessions. They had placed a saucer on one of the tables. An old

241

woman with a market bag mumbled a prayer in passing. She dropped a penny in the saucer. Other people
did the same. Each time the evicted family lowered
its eyes in shame. They were not beggars, but "re-
spectable" people. But if enough pennies fell in the
saucer, they might have rent for a new home. This
was the one hope left them.

Winter. Building a snow fort one morning, we boys
dug out a litter of frozen kittens and their mother.
The little ones were still blind. They had been born
into it, but had never seen our world.

Other dogs and cats were frozen. Men and women,
too, were found dead in hallways and on docks. Mary
Sugar Bum met her end in an alley. She was found
half-naked, clutching a whisky bottle in her blue claw.
This was her last "love" affair.

Horses slipped on the icy pavement, and quivered
there for hours with broken legs, until a policeman
arrived to shoot them.

The boys built a snow man. His eyes were two coals;
his nose a potato. He wore a derby hat and smoked a
corncob pipe. His arms were flung wide; in one of
them he held a broom, in the other a newspaper. This
Golem with his amazed eyes and idiotic grin amused
us all for an afternoon.

The next morning we found him strangely altered.
His eyes and nose had been torn out; his grin smashed,

like a war victim's. Who had played this joke? The
winter wind.

2

MRS. ROSENBAUM owned a grocery store on our
street. She was a widow with four children, and lived
in two rooms back of the store. She slaved from dawn
until midnight; a big, clumsy woman with a chapped
face and masses of untidy hair; always grumbling,
groaning, gossiping about her ailments. Sometimes she
was nervous and screamed at her children, and beat
them. But she was a kind-hearted woman, and that
winter suffered a great deal. Every one was very poor,
and she was too good not to give them groceries on
credit.

"I'm crazy to do it!" she grumbled in her icy store.
"I'm a fool! But when a child comes for a loaf of
bread, and I have the bread, and I know her family
is starving, how can I refuse her? Yet I have my own
children to think of! I am being ruined! The store is
being emptied! I can't meet my bills!"

She was kind. Kindness is a form of suicide in a
world based on the law of competition.

One day we watched the rewards of kindness. The
sheriff's men arrived to seize Mrs. Rosenbaum's grocery. They tore down the shelves and fixtures, they
carted off tubs of butter, drums of kerosene, sacks of
rice, flour and potatoes.

Mrs. Rosenbaum stood by watching her own funeral. Her fat kind face was swollen with crying as with toothache. Her eyes blinked in bewilderment. Her children clung to her skirts and cried. Snow fell from the sky, a crowd muttered its sympathy, a policeman twirled his club.

What happened to her after that, I don't know. Maybe the Organized Charities helped her; or maybe she died. O golden dyspeptic God of America, you were in a bad mood that winter. We were poor, and you punished us harshly for this worst of sins.

3

MY father lay in bed. His shattered feet ached in each bone. His painter's sickness came back on him; he suffered with lung and kidney pains.

He was always depressed. His only distraction was to read the Yiddish newspapers, and to make gloomy conversation at night over the suicides, the hungry families, the robberies, murders and catastrophes that newspapers record.

"It will come to an end!" said my father. "People are turning into wolves! They will soon eat each other! They will tear down the cities, and destroy the world in flames and blood!"

"Drink your tea," said my mother cheerfully, "God is still in the world. You will get better and work and laugh again. Let us not lose courage."

My father was fretful and nervous with an invalid's fears.

"But what if we are evicted, Katie?"

"We won't be evicted, not while I have my two hands and can work," said my mother.

"But I don't want you to work!" my father cried. "It breaks up our home!"

"It doesn't!" said my mother. "I have time and strength for everything."

4

AT first my mother had feared going out to work in a cafeteria among Christians. But after a few days she settled easily into the life of the polyglot kitchen, and learned to fight, scold, and mother the Poles, Germans, Italians, Irish and Negroes who worked there. They liked her, and soon called her "Momma," which made her vain.

"You should hear how a big black dishwasher named Joe, how he comes to me to-day, and says, 'Momma, I'm going to quit. Every one is against me here because I am black,' he says. 'The whole world is against us black people.'

"So I said to him, 'Joe, I am not against you. Don't be foolish, don't go out to be a bum again. The trouble with you here is you are lazy. If you would work harder the others would like you, too.' So he said, 'Momma, all right I'll stay.' So that's how it is in the restaurant. They call me Momma, even the black ones."

It was a large, high-priced cafeteria for businessmen on lower Broadway. My mother was a chef's helper, and peeled and scoured tons of vegetables for cooking. Her wages were seven dollars a week.

She woke at five, cooked our breakfast at home, then had to walk a mile to her job. She came home at five-thirty, and made supper, cleaned the house, was busy on her feet until bedtime. It hurt my father's masculine pride to see his wife working for wages. But my mother liked it all; she was proud of earning money, and she liked her fights in the restaurant.

My dear, tireless, little dark-faced mother! Why did she always have to fight? Why did she have to give my father a new variety of headache with accounts of her battles for "justice" in the cafeteria? The manager there was a fat blond Swede with a *Kaiserliche* mustache, and the manners of a Mussolini. All the workers feared this bull-necked tyrant, except my mother. She told him "what was what." When the meat was rotten, when the drains were clogged and smelly, or the dishwashers overworked, she told him so. She scolded him as if he were her child, and he listened meekly. The other workers fell into the habit of telling their complaints to my mother, and she would relay them to the Swedish manager.

'It's because he needs me," said my mother

proudly. "That's why he lets me scold him. I am one of his best workers; he can depend on me in the rush. And he knows I am not like the other kitchen help; they work a day or two; then quit, but I stay on. So he's afraid to fire me, and I tell him what is what."

It was one of those super-cafeterias, with flowers on the tables, a string orchestra during the lunch hour, and other trimmings. But my mother had no respect for it. She would never eat the lunch served there to the employees, but took along two cheese sandwiches from home.

"Your food is *Dreck*, it is fit only for pigs," she told the manager bluntly. And once she begged me to promise never to eat hamburger steak in a restaurant when I grew up.

"Swear it to me, Mikey!" she said. "Never, never eat hamburger!"

"I swear it, momma."

"Poison!" she went on passionately. "They don't care if they poison the people, so long as there's money in it. I've seen with my own eyes. If I could write English, I'd write a letter to all the newspapers."

"Mind your own business!" my father growled. "Such things are for Americans. It is their country and their hamburger steak."

5

OUR tenement was nothing but a junk-heap of rotten
lumber and brick. It was an old ship on its last
voyage; in the battering winter storms, all its seams
opened, and wind and snow came through.

The plaster was always falling down, the stairs
were broken and dirty. Five times that winter the
water pipes froze, and floods spurted from the plumbing, and dripped from the ceilings.

There was no drinking water in the tenement
for days. The women had to put on their shawls and
hunt in the street for water. Up and down the stairs
they groaned, lugging pails of water. In December,
when Mr. Zunzer the landlord called for rent, some
of the neighbors told him he ought to fix the plumbing.

"Next week," he murmured into his scaly beard.

"Next week!" my mother sneered, after he had
gone. "A dozen times he has told us that, the yellow-
faced murderer! May the lice eat him next week!
May his false teeth choke him to death next week!"

Some tenants set out hunting for other flats, but
could find none. The cheap ones were always occupied, the better flats were too dear. Besides, it wasn't
easy to move; it cost money, and it meant leaving
one's old neighbors.

"The tenements are the same everywhere, the landlords the same," said a woman. "I have seen places

to-day an Irisher wouldn't live in, and the rents are higher than here."

Toward the end of January, during a cataclysmic spell of snow, ice, and iron frost, the pipes burst again, and for weeks every one suffered for lack of water; the babies, old people, the sick ones. The neighbors were indignant. They gathered in the halls and held wild conversations. Mrs. Cracauer suggested that some one send in a complaint to the Board of Health. Mrs. Schuman said this was useless, the Board of Health belonged to Tammany Hall, and the landlord had a pull there.

Mrs. Tannenbaum exploded like a bomb of Jewish emotion. She was a worse agitator than my mother, a roly-poly little hysterical hippopotamus with a piercing voice.

"Let's all move out together!" she shrieked. "Let's get axes and hack out the walls and smash the windows and then move out!"

"No," said my mother, "I know something better."

Then and now, on the East Side, there have been rent strikes of tenants against their landlords. East Side tenants, I am sure, have always been the most obstreperous that ever gave a landlord sleepless nights and indigestion. My mother suggested a rent strike. The neighbors agreed with enthusiasm. They chattered about it in the weeks that followed. One told the other how she would curse the landlord when he came, and refuse to pay the rent.

"I'll spit in his face," said Mrs. Tannenbaum: "and tell him to kiss my *tochess* for his rent. Then I'll slam the door on him. That's what I'll do."

There spread through our tenement that feeling of exhilarating tension which precedes a battle. One counted the days until the first of February, when the landlord called for rent. What would he do? What would he say?

The hour came. Mrs. Tannenbaum, the fat, wild-eyed hippopotamus agitator, was the first tenant upon whose door the landlord knocked. She opened it meekly, paid the rent, and never spoke a word. Her husband had forbade her to make a fuss. He didn't want the bother of moving.

The next tenant, Mrs. Schuman across the hall, was so amazed at this treachery to the cause, that she paid her rent, too. Every one else paid, except my mother. She faced the landlord boldly, and said in a clear voice, for every one to hear:

"Fix first the plumbing, Mr. Zunzer, then I'll pay the rent."

Mr. Zunzer glared at her with his goggly eyes. For a minute he could not speak for rage. Then he yanked his red scrubby beard, and said:

"I'll throw you out! Mischief-maker. I know who

you are! You're the one who has been starting the rent strike here!"

"Yes," said my mother coolly. "And you've scared the others into paying you, but you can't scare me."

"I can't?" sputtered the landlord. "I will show you. To-morrow I'll call the sheriff and throw your furniture on the street!"

"No!" said my mother. "First you will have to take me to court! I know what my rights are!"

"*Pfoo* on your rights!" said the landlord. "I can do anything I want in this district. I have a pull with Tammany Hall!"

My mother put her hands on her hips, and asked him quietly: "But with God have you a pull, Mr. Zunzer?"

Mr. Zunzer was startled by this sally. He tried to meet it with haughtiness.

"Don't talk to me of God," he said. "I am more often in the synagogue than you and your husband together. I give a dozen times more money there."

"Every one knows you have money," said my mother quietly, "even the Angel of Death. Some day he will come for *all* your money, Mr. Zunzer."

The landlord's face paled; he trembled. He tried to speak, but the words choked him. He looked queer, as if he were about to faint. Then he pulled himself together, and walked away. My mother slammed the door after him, and laughed heartily. She rushed to the window, and called across the airshaft to Mrs. Ashkenazi and other neighbors. They had been sitting at their windows, listening greedily to the quarrel.

"Did you hear what hell I gave to that landlord? Didn't I give it to him good?"

"Madwoman!" my father called from the bedroom. "Where will we go when he puts us out to-morrow?"

"He won't put us out," said my mother confidently. "The landlord is scared of me, I could see it in his eyes."

My father sneered at her. Who ever heard of a landlord being scared of his tenant? But it was true this time; the landlord did not bother us again. He actually fixed the plumbing. He sent an agent to collect the rent. He was scared; my mother had made a lucky hit when she taunted him with the Angel of Death.

Mr. Zunzer was superstitious. His deepest fear was that burglars would break in some night and kill him and take his money. Dr. Solow told us the story one night:

6

"WHEN Mr. Zunzer first came to America," Dr. Solow related, "he peddled neckties, shoe laces and collar-buttons from a tray. He was very poor. He slept on a mattress in a cobbler's damp cellar, and lived on herrings and dry bread. He starved and suffered for five years. That's how he got the yellow face you see on him.

"Every penny he could grab he saved like a miser. He tied the nickels and dimes in a bag which he hid in a crack under his mattress. He worried. Big rats ran across his face while he slept. They did not bother him a tenth as much as did thoughts of his money.

"Oh, how sacred was that money to him. It was money to bring his wife and children from Europe. He was hungry for them. He would cry at night thinking about them. The money was not money; it was his family, his peace, his happiness, his life and death.

"One night some one stole this money from under the mattress. It was the savings of three years. Mr. Zunzer almost went crazy. He was sick in a hospital for months. He refused to eat. He wanted to die. But he took heart and commenced saving again. In two years he was able to send for his wife and children.

"Happiness did not come with them. Mr. Zunzer had formed the habit of saving money. He was a miser. He grudged his wife and children every cent they needed. He gave them little to eat. His wife fell sick; he grudged her a doctor. She died. At the funeral he fought with the undertaker over the burial price. He was always thinking of money.

"His children grew up hating him for his miserly ways. One by one they left him. The eldest boy became a thief. The second boy joined the U. S. Army. The girl disappeared.

"Mr. Zunzer was left alone. He is rich now, he

owns a pawnshop and several tenement houses. But he still lives on herring and dry bread, and saves pennies like a miser. It is a disease.

"He has fits," said Dr. Solow. "Every few months I am called to him. He is rolling on the floor, he knocks his head against furniture, he cuts his face on falling dishes. He screams robbers are killing him, and stealing his money. I talk to him quietly. I give him a medicine. I light the gas, to show him there are no burglars. All night I talk to him as to a child.

"About ten years ago a junkman he knew was murdered by thieves and robbed. Since then Mr. Zunzer has the fear the same thing will happen to him.

" 'Listen,' " I tell him, 'you must stop worrying about money. It is making you crazy, Mr. Zunzer.' "

"He wrings his hands, he weeps, and says to me: 'Yes, Dr. Solow, it is making me crazy. But what can I do? It is in my blood, in my heart. Can I cut it out of me with a knife?' "

" 'No,' I answer him, 'there are other ways, Mr. Zunzer.' "

" 'What other ways?' he weeps. 'Shall I throw my money in the river? Shall I give it to the synagogue? What good would it do? How can one live without money? And if other men fight for money, must one not fight, too? The whole world is sick with this disease, Dr. Solow, I am not the only one.' "

"So what can I answer? He will die in one of his

fits. His money will disappear down the sewer. Sometimes I am sorry for him; it's not altogether his fault. It *is* a world sickness. Even we who are not misers suffer from it. How happy the world would be without money! Yet what's to be done?"

My mother wagged her head mournfully through this tale of Mr. Zunzer's sickness. She said:

"The poor man! Maybe he needs another wife."

Ach, my mother! she could be sorry for any one, even a landlord.

7

YET she fought the landlord again that winter. The rent was due, and by a coincidence my brother, my sister, my mother and I all needed shoes. We had worn the old ones until they were in shreds. It was impossible to patch them any longer. My mother decided to pawn the family's diamond ring—the one my father had bought in a prosperous period.

I went with my mother to Mr. Zunzer's pawnshop. In summer it had swinging wicker doors like a saloon. Now we entered through heavy curtained doors that shut out the daylight.

It was a grim, crowded little store smelling of camphor. There were some gloomy East Side people standing around. The walls were covered with strange objects: guitars, shovels, blankets, clocks; with lace curtains, underwear and crutches; all these miserable trophies of the defeat of the poor.

Everything worth more than a quarter was taken in pawn by Mr. Zunzer, from an old man's false teeth to a baby's diapers. People were sure to redeem these little necessities. If he made ten cents on a transaction he was satisfied, for there were hundreds of them. At the end of a week there was a big total.

It was said in the neighborhood he also bought stolen things from the young thieves and pickpockets.

We waited for our turn. An old Irish worker in overalls, with merry blue eyes and a rosy face, was trying to pawn some tools. He was drunk, and pleaded that he be given a dollar. Mr. Zunzer gave him only half a dollar, and said, "Get the hell out." The white-haired Irishman jigged and sang as he left for the saloon.

A dingy little woman pawned a baby carriage. An old Jewish graybeard pawned his prayer book and praying shawl. A fat Polish woman with a blowsy, weepy face pawned an accordion. A young girl pawned some quilts; then our turn came.

The landlord wore a black alpaca coat in the pawnshop, and a skull cap. He crouched on a stool behind the counter. One saw only his scaly yellow face and bulging eyes; he was like an anxious spider. He picked up the ring my mother presented him, screwed a jeweler's glass into his eye, and studied it in the gaslight.

"Ten dollars," he said abruptly.

"I must have fifteen," said my mother.

"Ten dollars," said the landlord.

"No, fifteen," said my mother.

He looked up irritably and stared at her with his near-sighted eyes. He recognized her in the pawnshop gloom.

"You're my tenant, aren't you?" he asked, "the one that made all the trouble for me?"

"Yes," said my mother, "what of it?"

The landlord smiled bitterly.

"Nothing," he said, "but you are sure to come to a bad end."

"No worse end than yours," said my mother, "may the bananas grow in your throat!"

"Don't curse me in my own shop!" said the landlord. "I'll have you arrested. What do you want here?"

"I told you," said my mother, "I want fifteen dollars on this ring."

"It is worth only ten," said the landlord.

"To me you must give fifteen," said my mother boldly.

The landlord paled. He looked at my mother fearfully. She knew his secret. My mother mystified and alarmed him with her boldness. He was accustomed to people who cowered.

He wrote out a ticket for the ring, gave my mother fifteen dollars. She crowed over her victory as we

walked home. Next day she bought shoes for my
brother, my sister Esther, and myself. Her own shoes
she forgot to buy. That's the way she generally arranged things.

Chapter 19

~~~~~~

THE YOUNG AVENGERS

1

WINTER. Warm clothes, strong shoes, coal, food, so many costly necessities.

Winter. A blind beggar in the back yard: his face lifted to the snowy sky! Singing the vulgar smut of Yiddish music halls. He is hoarse, patient, old. People throw pennies to him, or hunks of bread wrapped in newspaper.

Winter. Children, old men and women fight like hungry dogs around a half-finished building. Waste lumber is being given away. A gaunt old Jewish woman drags a child's sled piled with lumber! stumbles, and picks up her old bones. She wipes her nose on her shawl, then tugs again at the rope.

Winter. Bums sleep in rows like dead fish on the sawdust floors of the saloons. It is long past midnight. In a ragpickers' basement five old Jewish men sit by a lamp and sort rags. One of them eats a sandwich.

Winter. In an Irish home a dead baby lies wrapped in a towel on the kitchen table. The father and mother sit side by side, quarrel, and guzzle whisky from a bottle.

Winter. An Italian child is sick with fever in a bedroom. Her eyes are swollen; a wet handkerchief

259

is tied around her forehead. But she must earn her living. She sits up in bed and works at artificial flowers—at lilies, roses and forsythia!

Winter. There are too many bodies to be buried in Potter's field. The city is forced to plant them in layers of three, to "save time and space," say the newspapers.

Winter. Snowball fights! We snowballed fat dignified men in derby hats, to see them grow angry. We made ice slides; we built bonfires on the pavement, and roasted potatoes until the cop chased us and stamped the fire out.

2

NIGGER, our leader, organized a secret league known as the "Young Avengers of Chrystie Street." Pishteppel, Jakie Gottlieb, and I and two others were the charter members with Nigger.

Our object was to avenge wrongs done to a member, and to hold pow-wows and roast sweet potatoes.

We built a house of old lumber and junk in the vacant lots of Delancey Street, and met there nights.

The house was entered by a secret tunnel. It contained two chairs, a mattress and a lantern, and had a chimney made of tomato cans.

The walls were plastered with newspaper pictures of baseball players and prize fighters, our heroes.

We took the Indian oath of fire and blood. We

pricked our thumbs and smeared the blood on the
paper. Then with a burning stick we branded our forearms with the mystic star.

I was the first member to be avenged. A big Irish
boy who sold newspapers at Houston Street and the
Bowery beat me up several times, and tore up my
papers. "I'll murder you, kid, if yuh peddle around
here again," he said.

The Young Avengers trailed me one afternoon. The
big Irish boy, as usual, rushed at me like a bulldog.
But the five of us fell upon him with whoops and cries,
punching and clawing in a pinwheel of gory excitement. We defeated him. It was the first victory for
the Young Avengers. There followed another.

3

Nigger's family was known as one of the poorest on
our street. He worried about them behind his grim
mask of a little Indian. But he never whimpered; his
lonely grief and pride were expressed in an abnormal
pugnacity.

Nigger's father was a "journeyman" tailor. He
sewed by hand the finest suits for the fashionable
Fifth Avenue shops. This work could not be done in
mass production by the large clothing factories. It
needed the skill of individual craftsmen.

But the pay was less than that earned by a girl
in an overall factory. The craftsmen had no trade

union. They were poor isolated immigrants working at home.

I will never forget Nigger's home; this place where were manufactured so many expensive suits for American judges, bankers and captains of industry.

Nigger was ashamed of it; and allowed none of the boys to call on him there. But one day my mother brought from the restaurant a box of eggs. She would have been indignant had any one said she was stealing them. She had merely taken them; the cafeteria was rich, it had wagonloads of eggs. Why would they miss a mere dozen or two? So she sent me with half the box to Nigger's family.

I came into a dingy gaslit room. I could see two smaller rooms leading off from it, gray and spidery dens. Every inch of the flat was crowded. There were beds everywhere; a family of seven lived here.

In a corner a sick child whimpered on a mattress. Near her face stood a chamber pot. The rooms were terrifically hot. Nigger was feeding the blazing stove with lumber he had just dragged in from the street.

Toys, newspapers, pieces of cloth and tailor's trimmings littered the floors. The walls were a poisonous green. Three calendars hung on the walls. One was a chromo showing Teddy Roosevelt charging up San Juan Hill; the most popular art work of the period. There was also a large crayon enlargement in a flyspeckled gold frame. It showed Nigger's father and mother on their wedding day; she standing in her white bridal veil, holding a bouquet; he sitting in solemn bridegroom's black at a table.

The photograph had been taken during their first year in America. The faces were young, naïve, European peasant faces.

The face Nigger's father turned upon me was fifteen years older. It was a skull with sharp cheek bones and nose from which the flesh had rotted as in a mummy. His eyes were large and strange. They reminded me of the eyes of a dog I had seen dying in the street.

"What do you want?" Nigger's father asked in a hoarse voice.

He sat crosslegged on a table under the gas jet, hunched in the working pose of tailors. He was sewing an expensive coat. A dirty rag was tied around his throat, and a towel around his forehead. God had given him a cancer. Its faint sickly violet smell mingled in the room with the stink of dirt, old lumber, chamber pot, bed linen, greasy dishes, and despair.

The man's eyes and his hoarse voice terrified me. I thought he was angry. I could not breathe in this hot room. I felt oppressed by it all, I couldn't tell why. I wanted to escape.

The tailor smiled at me kindly and wagged his head.

"Has the cat stolen your tongue?" he asked. "What is it, little one?"

His needle flashed in and out, sewing a millionaire's coat, and scenting it with the perfume of pauper's cancer.

I remained dumb. Nigger stepped forward belligerently, his fists doubled, as if he wanted to hit me. He resented my coming here; I could tell it in his gloomy eyes.

"What the hell do you want?" he said. "Talk up."

I found my voice at last. I produced the eggs and gave them to Nigger.

"My mother sent these eggs," I stammered.

There was a crash. A stout little woman in a kimono dashed in from the next room, upsetting chairs and dishes in her crazy haste. It was Nigger's mother. She flung her arms around me.

"Thank you, thank you, my darling!" she cried, smothering me with hysterical kisses. "May there be better days for all of us! May a fire burn up our enemies! They don't let me sleep at night, but I spit on them! I spit on them!"

I was appalled and bewildered.

"Malka," said the tailor quietly to his wife, "you are frightening the child. Abie, give your mother a glass of water. She is excited again."

The woman sat down and wiped her face with her apron. She drank the water, and panted with hysteria.

We watched her. Finally, she reached out and took the eggs from Nigger. Her voice now was very gentle. She stroked my hair.

"What a good woman your mother is!" she said. "Tell her we are thankful. And you, too, are a good boy to bring the eggs. Thanks, my darling."

I left Nigger's home shaken to the soul. I never forgot that scene. But to Nigger it was everyday life. His mother did queer things at times that were the talk of the neighborhood. She was half-insane; her misery had poisoned her, and made her too indignant. Only the passive are "sane."

4

LILY was five years older than her brother Nigger. She was an attractive child, with her soft olive face and great eyes. She was taken from school at an early age, and basted coats at home with her mother and another sister.

Two adults and three children worked incessantly in that family, and together never earned more than an average of $12 weekly during a year.

Lily hated the long dreary hours of work. Her only fun was snatched when she was sent to the Fifth Avenue shop to carry back the finished suits, or to fetch the unfinished materials.

She would put down her bundle on the sidewalk, and dance to every hand-organ she met. She could not resist this. Once her mother found the dark, gay little girl dancing, and grabbed her by the hair.

"Monster! So this is where you are! Take that and that!"

"But, momma, I want to play sometimes! I must have some play!"

"Play, play!" her mother screamed, "while at home we starve! How can we work if you do not bring us the coats, but dance in the street?"

She beat the child. Lily would not leave the hand-organ. There was a frantic, ugly scene between the mother and child. At last the mother subdued her, and the sobbing child said, "Yes, I'll go home."

They looked around for the bundle of coats Lily had been carrying. It had disappeared. A Bowery bum had stolen it during the excitement. He would probably sell it at some pawnshop for a dollar. Nigger's mother went out of her mind. For months she was hysterical day and night. But even in her delirium she worked, and drove the others on to work faster. The lost bundle had to be paid for.

Nigger was sent to the shops with bundles after that. Lily could not be trusted. She might play again. For years she was kept indoors all day, basting coats. At the age of fifteen she rebelled. She went to work in a paper box factory. She began to wear long dresses, and put up her hair. She flirted with boys in the hallways; she went to dances and stayed out late at night.

Her parents scolded her; but she fought back, she was earning wages, she was free at last.

One night, after a terrific quarrel in which her mother tried to beat the grown-up girl, Lily ran out of the house and didn't come back. The mother hunted for her everywhere, but couldn't find her. Weeks passed, Lily didn't appear.

Then some one saw her walking on 14th Street, with Louis One Eye. She was powdered and painted, and swung the insouciant little handbag of a prostitute. Her name was never mentioned again in Nigger's home.

Nigger said nothing. But one night, at a meeting of the Young Avengers around our campfire, he stood up and said: "Foller me, gang."

We obeyed. He led us to the roof of the tenement where Louis One Eye kept his pigeons.

There, in the moonlight, we crawled on our bellies to the pigeon house, and broke the lock.

We entered and cut the throats of forty pigeons.

They fluttered their wings as we murdered them, then lay silent and gory.

The thick snow glittered on the roof. Skyscrapers vibrated in the distance. A black cat prowled in the snow.

We whispered to each other, and stared about us, expecting Louis. Our hands reeked with blood.

5

LOUIS ONE EYE may have suspected Nigger of the crime but never tried to punish him for it.

When the boy and the man met, however, they glared at each other like enemies.

Nigger's sister called at the home once to see the children, whom she loved. The parents wouldn't talk to her.

Nigger's father died. Lily came to the funeral, but her mother refused to speak to her even then.

Lily sent money to the family by mail, and they spent it, but never answered her letters.

Once Nigger and I met her on the street, and she laughed and tried to talk to us. Nigger walked away. Lily died in a hospital at the age of nineteen, of what the East Side called "the black syphilis."

Seven years later, when Nigger grew up, one of his first deeds as a gangster was to kill Louis One Eye.

CHAPTER 20

BLOOD MONEY

1

THE livery stable was a busy scene of life and
death. It was a depot for wedding and funeral
coaches, and headquarters for the Callahan Transfer
Express.

The expressmen were leather-faced young Irish,
the coach drivers were leather-faced young Jews.

Between jobs these citizens of the two leading
persecuted and erratic small nations of the world
loafed on a bench. They fought, philosophized and
drank buckets of beer together in the sunlight.

Their bench was on the sidewalk in front of the
stable. There were always ten or twelve drivers sitting
here, and at least one gay little whore and a goat or
a dog.

The stable was an antique five-storied brick building standing next to my own tenement. In summer
the place stank, it was a dynamo generating bad
smells. It added, to the ripe odors of my street, the
rare attar of rotting manure. It poisoned my sleep. It
was beloved by millions of flies. They grew fat and
putrid in the stable, then visited my home.

Giant orchids grow in the South American jungles.

I have seen them; some weigh hundreds of pounds. Their manure-fragrance makes them a magnet to whole nations of flies. And the Indians fear these orchids. They occasionally collapse on a sleeping man, and kill him. Our stable had its victims, too, but no one realized this except young Dr. Solow, who hated flies, and warned us against them.

2

I LIKED to go on funerals with the Jewish coach drivers. What glorious summer fun. Nathan was a tall Jewish ox, with a red hard face like a chunk of rusty iron. His blustering manner had earned him many a black eye and bloody face. It was a warm bright morning. Three coaches rolled down the ramp of the livery stable, on their way to a funeral. Then appeared Nathan, cursing at his horses. I begged him to let me go along. He was grouchy, but slowed down. I scrambled up beside him on the tall seat.

Three coaches and a hearse. A poor man's funeral. We rolled through the hurly-burly East Side. The sporty young drivers joked from coach to coach. The horses jerked and skipped, Nathan cursed them.

"You she-devil," he said in Yiddish to his white horse, "steady down, or I'll kick in your belly!"

He tugged at the check-rain and cut her mouth until it bled. But she was nervous; horses have their moods.

We came to the tenement of the corpse. Many pushcarts had to be cursed out of the way. We lined the curb. There was a crowd gathered. Funerals, weddings, sewer repairs, accidents, fires and love-murders, food of the crowd.

The coffin was brought down by four pale men with black beards. Then came the wife and children in black, meekly weeping. The family were so poor they had not the courage to weep flamboyantly.

But some of the neighbors did. It was their pleasure. They made an awful hullabaloo. It pierced one's marrow. The East Side women have a strange keening wail, it is very Gaelic. They chant the virtues of the dead sweatshop slave, and the sorrow of his family. They fling themselves about in an orgy of grief. It unpacks their hearts, but is hell on bystanders.

3

THEN the ride across the Brooklyn Bridge, with the incredible sweep of New York below us. The river was packed tight, a street with tugboat traffic. Mammoth skyscrapers cut into the sky like a saw. The smoke of factories smeared the bright blue air. Horns boomed and wailed; Brooklyn lay low and passive in the horizon.

"A man is crazy to live in Brooklyn," said Nathan, pointing with his whip toward that side. "My God, it is dead as a cemetery; no excitement, no nothing

Look, Mikey, down there. That's the Navy Yard.
That's where they keep the American warships.
Sailors are a lot of Irish bums. Once I had a fight
with a sailor and knocked his tooth out. He called me
a Jew."

"Ain't you a Jew?" I asked timidly, as my greedy
eyes drank in the panorama.

"Of course I'm a Jew," said Nathan, in his rough,
iron voice, "I'm proud I'm a Jew, but no Irish bum
can call me names, or call me a Jew."

"Why?" I asked.

I was very logical when I was seven years old.

"Why?" Nathan mimicked me with a sneer. "Why?
You tell a kid something, and he asks why? Kids give
me a headache." Nathan spat his disgust into the
river. The blob of spit fell a third of a mile.

4

THEY put the coffin into the ground. The old Rabbi in
a shiny high hat chanted a long sonorous poem in
Hebrew, a prayer for dead Jews. A woman screamed;
it was the dead man's wife. She tried to throw herself
into the grave. Her weeping friends restrained her.
The graveyard trees waved strangely. The graveyard
sun was strange. The grave diggers shoveled earth
into the grave. I felt lonesome and bewildered. I
wanted to cry like the rest, but was ashamed because
of Nathan.

Then it was over. All of us went to a restaurant at the entrance to the cemetery and ate platters of sour cream, pot cheese and black bread, the Jewish funeral food. Even the widow ate. Nathan gave me half of his portion. Then we rode home over the Bridge.

I was glad to feel the East Side again engulf our coach. I lost my vague funeral loneliness in the hurly-burly of my street. On the stoop of our tenement sat two friends, my sister Esther and Nigger's little sister Leah. In the purple and golden light of sundown they were reading a fairy-tale book and eating bread and butter. Their faces were calm and satisfied. But I made them envious.

"Nathan took me on another funeral ride," I crowed, "and I saw another man buried."

The girls were gratifyingly envious. Girls were never taken on these rides by the coach drivers. My sister Esther always wanted to go, but couldn't. She blamed me for it, and said I told the drivers not to take her. She cried now, as I teased her, and described to her how wonderful my adventure had been. She grew very jealous of my good luck. My poor dear little sister! so soon to go on that funeral ride, and not return and boast like me!

5

IN that evil winter that had fallen on us my sister Esther did most of the housework while my mother was at the restaurant. The child bought groceries, she cooked, scrubbed floors, and watched our baby brother. She was my father's nurse. Once, I remember, she stood by his bedside and fondly stroking his hair, said, like some kind, beautiful woman:

"Poppa, I'm sorry you are sick. How I wish no one in the world was ever sick! But you'll be better soon; don't worry, poppa dear!"

My father clasped her to him, and kissed her eyes and mouth and hands, and called her every Yiddish name of love: his Moon, his Wealth, his Little Mother, his Rose, his Tiny Dove, his Heart of Hearts.

There was so much energy in that meager body with its long twinkling sparrow legs. There was so much affection in the great soft eyes. Esther was not driven to the housework: she herself saw its necessity, and did it with sunny cheerfulness. She wished to help my mother. She wished to help everybody; she was precociously kind.

Esther was dreamy, too; she read every book of fairy-tales, and believed in them. She was always making up new games to play, and inventing mythical characters. After she read a book she would repeat it in detail to my father, who loved any kind of story. I was a year older, but felt like a man beside Esther. When I told her the things I knew about our East Side street, she would cry, and say I was lying to her. I despised her weakness.

Why did I always fight with my sister? Why did I refuse to do the chores about the house but shifted them all to her shoulders? I remember one evening when I came in from my newspaper peddling my father asked me to go out again and find some wood for the stove. I refused and made a scene. I said Esther ought to do it. Esther was busy with a dozen other things, and said so. I called her names, and sulked. She only shrugged her shoulders at my stubbornness, and went out quietly to hunt for the stove-wood.

I was always winning these easy victories over her.

6

ONCE my little sister sat on the tenement stoop, reading the Blue Fairy Tale Book. This book was her treasure. It was a big beautiful edition with colored pictures that Harry had given her. She had copied many of those pictures with her crayons, and knew every story in the book by heart. But she loved to read them again and again, her lips moving dreamily, as if she were singing to herself. She was reading now on the stoop, while the New York sun burned out above the tenements in glorious purple, amber and rose.

Esther was in her own world. The street whirled and clashed around her, the gray old solemn Jews went by, and gabbling mommas, and pimps, pushcarts and rattling wagons. A scabby dog rummaged with its front paws in a garbage can. Three tough guys lounged nearby, and quarreled, and spat tobacco juice. The saloon was busy, the prostitutes were busy, the slum wretchedness was huge and triumphant. But Esther had escaped from it all. She was reading her book. The twilight fell on the white pages and illuminated her face.

She looked up as I approached. I can still see the flushed little face, with its Jewish cheek bones, ardent mouth, and large eyes. She looked at me and did not see me. She was lost in the land of fairies and giants, where children talked familiarly with swans and lions, and sought enchanted castles beyond the mountains of glass.

Fiend that I was, I snatched her away from that beautiful, magic land. I tore the book from her hands, and ran off with it, yelling cruel taunts. I wanted to torture her. I wanted to make her cry.

Forgive me now, Esther.

Another time I beat her until her nose bled. She had followed me into the secret fort of the Young Avengers, and had shamed me before my comrades, by saying that momma wanted me at home.

Another time I grabbed all the lovely fruit and candy Dr. Solow had brought us, and gobbled up her share as well as mine. She cried because I could be so selfish and greedy: she was never greedy.

7

The winter dragged on, that gloomiest of winters. My father moped and smoked about the house; my mother worked in the restaurant; I peddled papers after school; and loyal little Esther did the housework.

My aunt left our home. Dr. Solow was busy; he did not call so often to drink tea with us in the evenings.

Nothing else changed. Nothing else happened.

Until late one winter afternoon.

8

The world was dark. Snow smothered the city, the streets and tenements.

An Arctic midnight seemed to have usurped the day. It was strange to see so many lamps burning at noon. In school the lights were on. In the streets the stores and skyscrapers were illuminated. Along the Bowery when I peddled my papers I found the saloons blazing with gas and electricity.

The snow never stopped falling in this unnatural darkness. It was dreadful to be outdoors. One could see nothing, except queer looming shapes of horses and men plowing head-on through the snow. Toward five I was so exhausted that I decided to go home. Half my papers were unsold, but I was too frozen and blind to carry on.

When I reached home I found my mother there.

The cafeteria had closed down early. My mother was exhausted by her half-mile walk from the street car. She had taken off her wet shoes, and was drying her stockings by the stove.

"Where is Esther?" she asked when I came in.

"I don't know," I said. "I haven't seen her all day."

"Herman, where is Esther?" my mother called in a louder voice.

"She has gone out to gather wood for the stove," answered my father from the bedroom.

My mother shook her head, moodily.

"Too bad," she said. "It is the devil's own weather."

The soup pot was boiling on the stove, set there by my sister Esther. There was a pot of stewing prunes, and the tea kettle. She had laid, too, the table with plates, forks and spoons for supper. The rooms were tidy; she had done the housework before leaving to forage for wood.

"Pst, the poor child, she has on such a thin jacket," said my mother. "I am sorry she went out."

I took off my own shoes and hung up my stockings to dry. I counted my money; I had earned only nineteen cents that miserable day of lead. I sat down to read a Henty tale before supper. After supper I would do my school home work. My mother hobbled with bare feet into the bedroom to look at the baby and talk to my father.

I plunged into my Henty book, and forgot every-

thing else. It was a story of Richard Cœur de Lion.
Then my mother interrupted the glorious tale. She
leaned over my shoulder and asked nervously:

"So where is Esther? Hasn't she come yet?"

"No, momma."

"Pst! I am beginning to be worried. It is such a
bad day! Maybe I ought to go out and find her. She
may need help with the wood, my poor dove."

My mother began to draw on her stockings. Then
she put on her shoes, and fussed about the kitchen
before she wrapped herself in her big shawl. She had
the shawl in her hand when three knocks sounded at
the door. They were so violent that my mother and I
both started in dread.

"Come in," said my mother, transfixed with the
shawl about her.

The door was flung open. We were amazed to
see a crowd of strange people in the hallway. They
seemed fantastic in the gaslight, with their white faces
and staring eyes. Their overcoats and hats were covered with snow. A tall, stout man with a black mustache was sobbing fiercely. The others stood stark as
ghosts.

My mother held her heart.

"Quick, what has happened?" she asked.

A woman in the crowd shrieked. The crowd stirred
uneasily at this, but was still mute. A little round-

shouldered man with glasses stepped forward and apologized:

"Don't be excited, missus; the doctor will soon come."

"What doctor? What has happened? Tell me!" my mother demanded.

But the snow-laden people stared at her, and could not speak. Their lips were locked, as in a nightmare. They stared at us strangely. Then they parted and through their midst walked a pale man dressed in a grocer's apron. He was sweating with nervousness, and his eyes blinked. In his arms he carried the body of a little girl. She was dripping with blood. Some of it dabbled on the grocer's apron and hands.

"Esther!" my mother moaned. "Esther!"

All the ghostly people began to cry. Some turned their faces away, or covered their eyes in pain. The grocer laid Esther across a table. Her head fell back. Her eyes were shut, her face crushed and bloody.

"My darling, my flower, what have they done to you?" my mother wailed. She tried to fling herself on Esther. An old woman gently held her by the shoulder.

My mother wet a towel and wiped the blood from Esther's face. The little face was mutilated with deep wounds, as by a butcher's cleaver. My mother kissed her and kissed her again. My father came from the bedroom and howled like an animal. He fell on his knees and chafed Esther's cold hands.

My mother was walking up and down in a daze, wringing her hands.

"How did it happen? How did it happen?"

A babble of tearful voices broke out to tell her. Esther had been dragging her sled with its load of wood. She was crossing the street at our own corner, when in the blinding snow-fog an Adams Express truck hit her. She fell between the horses and the heavy wheels rolled over her body.

"My baby, my treasure!" wept my mother.

"Esther, talk to me! Open your eyes and look at poppa! Look, I have some candy for you, Esther, and a new picture book!" my father implored on his knees.

"Where is the doctor?" my mother cried frantically.

"He is coming soon. A telephone was sent him," a woman murmured in the crowd.

The truck-driver appeared. He was a burly blond young German-American in a big overcoat fastened at the neck with a safety pin. He took off his fur cap and heavy snow fell from it to the floor. He stared about him with bewildered eyes. His broad face, red and raw as beefsteak with the cold wind, was twisted grotesquely, like a baby's that wants to cry.

"Honest to God," he said, "I couldn't see her with all that snow! The first thing I knew she was under the wheels."

My father leaped up and grabbed the unfortunate driver by the throat.

"Murderer!" my father shouted.

The driver did not attempt to defend himself, but wept.

"Honest!" he sobbed, "I'm a father myself, I got two kids of my own, mister, but I couldn't see her because of all the snow, so help me Christ!"

My father was torn away from the driver's throat. Every one could see the poor driver was not to blame. People kept washing Esther's face and talking to her. But she did not answer them. A frightened boy brought in the sled with all the wood she had gathered. The room was hot; the people packed it tightly, and groaned and talked; the gaslight flickered.

"My baby, my baby!" wailed my mother, walking up and down the room, and striking her breast. My father sat by Esther as if in a trance.

Then a young doctor in white ducks appeared. He took Esther away in his ambulance to the hospital. There she died during the night, without a word.

9

ALL the night Esther lay in her coffin on the table in the "front room." While she slept, old men hired at the synagogue sat by candlelight in our kitchen. They read Hebrew prayers until dawn. I would wake in the middle of the night, and see their huge shadows

swaying on the airshaft walls. And I heard the murmur of their voices, and my father and mother groaning in sleep, and life oppressed me with its mystery and terror.

My little sister was *dead*. A boy does not know what the word means, but he knows the solemnity, and the horror with which it affects the grown-ups around him. I had never seen my mother so frantic.

When my little sister was put into the earth, my mother tried to fling herself into the open grave beside her. She was restrained by my father. Every one wept as the Rabbi intoned the long Hebrew prayer for the dead. I wept, too, for I was beginning to understand why people cried at funerals, though afterward they ate black bread and pot cheese at the cemetery restaurant.

During the next week my parents did *Sheva*. They sat on the floor in stockinged feet, as is prescribed, and swayed from side to side and read the Hebrew ritual. Neighbors drifted in and out, cooked our meals, took care of us.

Joy and grief were social in a tenement. The neighbors crept in, one by one, and sat with us during the *Sheva*. There were mournful groups all day in the darkened rooms.

They offered my mother the most dismal comfort. Why is there so much gloomy wisdom at the hearts of the poor?

"My sister lost a little boy in the same way," said Mrs. Lipoff, a pickle vendor's wife. "That little Morris, such a dear child, would have been seven years old now; but a street car had to kill him. Yet what can we do? It is happening every day."

"Yes," my mother mumbled.

The janitress, her fat, honest face smeared with dirt and tears, said bitterly:

"I know a Galicianer family on Columbia Street. This year they lost a girl of Esther's age. The mother saw it happen. She was standing at the window, watching the child play in the street. Then the wagon came upon the child. The mother tore her hair out for sorrow. It is a shame on America! In Russia we could not live for the pogroms, but here our children are killed!"

"Yes," my mother said.

Reb Samuel's tiny wife bowed her head, and with the corner of her apron wiped her granulated eyelids. Then in her weak, kindly voice, she said:

"Yet what can we do? The children must play somewhere."

"Yes," my mother agreed.

My mother answered only yes and no to people; she was stunned; she did not seem to feel anything. She sat on the floor, rocking herself from side to side, and pressing to her nose a handkerchief wet with vinegar. Esther was dead.

10

A STRANGER called one day during the *Sheva*. He bustled in, a swarthy powerful man, with a coarse face, lobster eyes and short crooked legs. He looked like a gorilla, but was expensively dressed and amazingly suave. He took off his overcoat, laid it carefully over the back of a chair, and adjusted his diamond horseshoe scarfpin. Then he shook my father's hand and my mother's.

"My sincere regrets over your accident," he said with an undertaker's false, fluent pathos. "It is terrible to lose a child, especially for a mother. I am a parent myself; I know what you must feel."

He fished into his pockets and handed a business card to my father, and one to my mother. They regarded the cards dully. The stranger seemed to overpower them.

"As you will read," he went on glibly, "I am Mr. Jonas Schlessel, the well-known attorney-at-law. I am also a close friend of Mr. Baruch Goldfarb, the ward leader, who told me you were his friend, too. Eh, what a great man, a great man! Well, my friends, to come to the point, I have been studying this accident that has happened to you. I have decided you have a fine damage suit against the Adams Express. It ought to be good for a thousand dollars! I am willing to represent you, because you are friends of Mr. Goldfarb. You do not have to pay me anything now; only when I have won the case. All you have to do now is sign this paper. So let us have it signed, and then I will proceed with the case. It means a thousand dollars, my friends!"

He flashed a legal document before my father. My father sat there stupefied. He took the paper, and the fountain pen the lawyer handed him, and seemed ready to sign like an automaton.

But my mother broke into sobs. "Go away!" she said to the lawyer. "I don't want you in my house!"

Mr. Schlessel looked at her in surprise.

"What's the matter?" he asked, spreading his hands.

"I don't want your blood money!" my mother wept.

The lawyer was deeply offended.

"Blood money?" he repeated. "Why is it blood money? It is accident money! I handle hundreds such cases every year."

He tried to argue with my mother, but she became hysterical and began to abuse him. So with an outraged air, he picked up his overcoat and opened the door.

"With greenhorns I never argue," he said loftily, as he left.

My father sat there in the same stupor that had seized him when the stranger entered.

"I don't know, Katie," he said slowly. "Maybe we

should take this money. God knows we need it now. I could start my shop with it. The child is gone, and nothing we do one way or the other makes any difference to our poor dove. So why—"

"Silence!" my mother said. "It is my feeling!"

My father was too bewildered and crushed by everything to answer her. He realized, too, from past experience that for some of her "feelings" my mother was ready to go to the stake. This evidently was one of the times. Esther was dead.

CHAPTER 21

BANANAS

1

ESTHER was dead. My mother had borne every-thing in life, but this she could not bear. It frightened one to see how quiet she became. She was no longer active, cheerful, quarrelsome. She sat by the window all day, and read her prayer book. As she mumbled the endless Hebrew prayers, tears flowed silently down her face. She did not speak, but we knew why she was crying. Esther was dead.

For months she was sunk in this stupor. She forgot to cook or sweep. My father and I had to do things. She was afraid, too, that I might be killed by a truck, and would not let me go out peddling the newspapers. She clung fiercely to my little brother and me and devoured us with kisses, and kept us beside her for hours. My father watched her anxiously during her long, gloomy apathies by the window.

"Katie, what is wrong?" he implored. "Katie, of what are you thinking?"

"Nothing," she said drearily. "I am only watching the children at play in the street."

"But you mustn't!" my father cried. "It reminds you of Esther! You will make yourself sick, Katie!"

288

"Let me be sick," she said. "Let me go out of
this world. One loves a child for years, then a truck
kills it."

My father shook his head mournfully. What could
he say to comfort her? Esther was dead. Words were
futile. It is twenty years since Esther was killed, but
my mother is still unconsoled. She visits the cemetery
once a month and scatters flowers over Esther's grave.
She still weeps for her child. It is as if Esther had
died yesterday; my mother will never be consoled.

2

WITH my mother so helpless, my father had to crawl
off his sickbed to hunt for work. But he found nothing. He asked here and there in a faint-hearted way.
It did no good. He was sick, discouraged, and could
speak no English. He was unskilled at any trade but
house painting, and his obsessive fear of climbing on
a scaffold shut him out of this work. There was little
else he could do. He walked the streets gloomily.

It is hard to say how we lived during the next year.
Out of every ten Americans one is a pauper, who
applies for help to organized charity. There is another
pauper tenth that is too proud for such begging. We
were in the latter tenth.

I can't describe how we managed to live. Does the
survivor remember everything from the time when

the ship founders until he is washed up on the beach?
All I know is we went on living.

The neighbors helped us. They brought in portions
of their suppers, and paper bags containing sugar,
coffee, beans, flour. Jake Wolf the saloonkeeper
quietly paid our rent for months. Other people were
kind. Once Rosie the prostitute placed a crumpled
five-dollar bill in my hand.

"Give this to your mother," she said. "Tell her you
found it in the street."

I tried to relay this lie to my mother, but broke
down under questioning. My mother sighed.

"Give Rosie my heartfelt thanks," she said. "Say
we will pay it back some day. But don't tell your
poppa; he is too proud."

Big Tim Sullivan the Tammany Hall leader sent
us a basket on Thanksgiving Day, stuffed with nuts,
candies, cranberries, celery, and a huge, blue-skinned
turkey.

"What kind of a holiday is it, this Thanksgiving?"
my mother asked.

I, the scholar of the family, told her it was the day
the Pilgrims had given thanks to God for America.

"So it's an American holiday," my mother said,
"and not for Jews."

The turkey was a fine fat bird, but unfortunately
of heathen origin. It was not *kosher*, and therefore
forbidden to us. We eyed it with longing, but my

father sold the turkey to one of the Irish bartenders
in Jake's saloon.

3

"I MUST do something! I must find some work! We
are starving!" my father would cry, beating his breast
with both fists in despair.

The neighbors tried to help us, but they themselves
were poor. Some well-meaning neighbor secretly
mailed a post card to the Charity society, telling of
our plight.

One day a stranger called. He was a slim fair-
haired, young Christian with a brisk hurry-up manner
and a stylish collar and necktie. He placed his umbrella against the wall, and shuffled through a bunch
of index cards. He had a bad cold, and was forever
blowing the most startling bugle-calls with his nose.

"Does Herman Gold live here?" he asked, sniffling
irritably.

"Yes, sir," said my mother.

She was very respectful, for this was evidently one
of the brusque young men who came from the Board
of Health, or the Public School, or the Christian
missions, or the settlement houses. They asked many
questions, and one must answer them or go to jail.

"I am from the United Charities," said this young
man, "and some one wrote us about you. We will
help you if you will answer some questions. How
many children have you?"

"Two," said my mother.

"How old?"

"One is six, the other ten."

"Husband sick?"

"Yes, sir."

"Private doctor or free clinic?"

"Private."

"Where do you get the money to pay him?"

"We, we——" my mother began.

The young investigator was making rapid notations on an index card. His eyes swept the room as he talked, as if he were tabulating every pot, pan, dishcloth and stick of furniture in our home. He interrupted my mother in her long explanation of our relations with Dr. Solow.

"And so your husband is out of work? Is he kind to you? Does he drink? What salary does he receive while working? Does he smoke? Has he tried to find a job recently? Does he ever beat you? How much of his salary does he give you when he is working? What rent do you pay? How much do your groceries cost per week?"

My mother was flustered by this Niagara of questions. She resented the brisk stranger who came into her home and asked personal questions with such an air of authority. But he was an official. She cleared her throat, and was about to give him his answers, when my father stalked in.

He had been resting in the bedroom, and was half-undressed. His face was pale, he trembled with rage. He glared at the young blond question-asker, and shouted:

"Get out of this house, mister! You have no business here. It is true we are poor, but that does not give you the right to insult us."

"I am not insulting you," said the young investigator, blowing his nose and shuffling his index cards nervously, "I ask these questions in about fifty homes a day. It is just the regular form."

My father drew himself up proudly.

"I spit on your regular form," he said. "We don't want any charity; we can live without it, mister."

"Very well," said the young man, gathering up his umbrella, his overcoat, his index cards, and making briskly for the door. "I'll report what you just said." He paused a moment to scratch a few more notes; then, blowing a last bugle-call on his damp nose, scurried down the hall. What he reported on his cards we never knew, but we were spared the indignity of any further visits by Organized Charity. Every one on the East Side hated and feared that cruel machine that helped no one without first systematically degrading him and robbing him of all human status. One's neighbors were kinder. Tammany Hall was kinder. Starvation was kinder. There were thousands of families like ours that would rather have died

than be bullied, shamed and finger-printed like criminals by the callous policemen of Organized Charity.

4

THE neighbors were talking about us. They were
worrying. In the tenement each woman knew what
was cooking for supper in her neighbor's pot. Each
knew the cares, too, that darkened a neighbor's heart.

One night a neighbor called. He kissed the
mezzuzah over the door, and wiped his feet on the
burlap rags. Then he timidly entered our kitchen like
an intruder.

"Good evening, Mr. Lipzin," said my mother.
"Please sit down."

"Good evening," he stammered, seating himself.
"It was raining to-day, and I did not sell many
bananas, so I brought you some. Maybe your children
like bananas."

He handed my mother a bunch of bananas, and she
took them, saying: "Thanks, Mr. Lipzin."

The pot-bellied little peddler shyly fingered his
beard. He had come for a purpose, but was too em-
barrassed to speak. Sweat appeared on his red, fat,
honest face, which wind and sun had tanned. He
scratched his head, and stared at us in a painful
silence. Minutes passed.

"How is your health, Mr. Lipzin?" my mother
asked.

"I am stronger, thanks be to God," he said bash-
fully. "It was only the rheumatism again."

"That is good. And how is your new baby, Mr.
Lipzin?"

"God be thanked, she is strong like a tiger," he
said.

He fell dumb again. He tapped his knees with his
fingers, and his shoulders twitched. He was known
as a silent man in the tenement; in the ten years
we lived there this was the first time he had called
on us.

My father fidgeted uneasily. He was about to say
something to break the spell cast by the tongue-tied
peddler, when Mr. Lipzin became articulate. "Excuse
me, but my wife nagged me into coming here," he
stammered. "She is worrying about you. Excuse me,
but they say you have been out of work a long time
and can find nothing to do, Mr. Gold."

"Yes, Mr. Lipzin, why should one conceal it?" said
my father. "Life is dark for us now."

"*Nu,*" said the little peddler, as he wiped his forehead, "so that is why my wife nagged me to see you.
If there is nothing else, one can at least make a kind
of living with bananas. I have peddled them, with
God's help, for many years. It is a hard life, but one
manages to live.

"Yes," he went on, in a mournful, hesitant singsong, "for a few dollars one buys a stock of bananas

from the wholesalers on Attorney Street. Then one
rents a pushcart for ten cents a day from the pushcart
stables on Orchard Street. Then one finds a street
corner and stands there and the people come and buy
the bananas."

"So well?" my father demanded, a hostile glare
in his eyes.

The little peddler saw this, and was frightened
again into incoherence.

"Excuse me, one makes a living, with God's help,"
he managed to say.

My father stood up and folded his arms haughtily.

"And you are suggesting, Mr. Lipzin, that I, too,
should go out peddling bananas?" he asked.

The peddler sweated like a runner with embarrassment. He stood up and edged toward the door to make
his escape.

"No, no, God forbid," he stammered. "Excuse me,
it was my wife who nagged me to come here. No, no,
Mr. Gold! Good evening to you all; may God be with
you!"

He went out, mopping his fiery face with a bandanna. My father stared after him, his arms still
folded in that fierce, defiant attitude.

"What a gall! What meddling neighbors we have!
To come and tell me that I ought to peddle these
accursed bananas! After my fifteen years in America,
as if I were a greenhorn! I, who once owned a sus-

pender shop, and was a foreman of house painters!
What do you think of such gall, Katie?"

"I don't know," said my mother quietly. "It is
not disgraceful to make an honest living by peddling."

"You agree with him?" my father cried.

"No," said my mother, "but Mr. Lipzin is a good
man. He came here to help you, and you insulted
him."

"So you do agree with him!" my father stormed.
He stamped indignantly into the bedroom, where he
flung himself on the bed and smoked his pipe viciously. My mother sighed, then she and my brother
and I ate some of the bananas.

5

My proud father. He raved, cursed, worried, he held
long passionate conversations with my mother.

"Must I peddle bananas, Katie? I can't do it; the
disgrace would kill me!"

"Don't do it," my mother would say gently. "We
can live without it."

"But where will I find work?" he would cry. "The
city is locked against me! I am a man in a trap!"

"Something will happen. God has not forgotten us,"
said my mother.

"I will kill myself! I can't stand it! I will take the
gas pipe to my nose! I refuse to be a peddler!"

"Hush, the children will hear you," said my mother.

I could hear them thrashing it out at night in the bedroom. They talked about it at the supper table, or sat by the stove in the gloomy winter afternoons, talking, talking. My father was obsessed with the thought of bananas. They became a symbol to him of defeat, of utter hopelessness. And when my mother assured him he need not become a peddler, he would turn on her and argue that it was the one way out. He was in a curious fever of mixed emotions.

Two weeks after Mr. Lipzin's visit he was in the street with a pushcart, peddling the accursed bananas.

He came back the first night, and gave my mother a dollar bill and some silver. His face was gray; he looked older by ten years; a man who had touched bottom. My mother tried to comfort him, but for days he was silent as one who has been crushed by a calamity. Hope died in him; months passed, a year passed; he was still peddling bananas.

I remember meeting him one evening with his pushcart. I had managed to sell all my papers and was coming home in the snow. It was that strange, portentous hour in downtown New York when the workers are pouring homeward in the twilight. I marched among thousands of tired men and women whom the factory whistles had unyoked. They flowed

in rivers through the clothing factory districts, then
down along the avenues to the East Side.

I met my father near Cooper Union. I recognized
him, a hunched, frozen figure in an old overcoat
standing by a banana cart. He looked so lonely, the
tears came to my eyes. Then he saw me, and his face
lit with his sad, beautiful smile—Charlie Chaplin's
smile.

"Ach, it's Mikey," he said. "So you have sold your
papers! Come and eat a banana."

He offered me one. I refused it. I was eleven years
old, but poisoned with a morbid proletarian sense of
responsibility. I felt it crucial that my father *sell* his
bananas, not give them away. He thought I was shy,
and coaxed and joked with me, and made me eat the
banana. It smelled of wet straw and snow.

"You haven't sold many bananas to-day, pop," I
said anxiously.

He shrugged his shoulders.

"What can I do? No one seems to want them."

It was true. The work crowds pushed home
morosely over the pavements. The rusty sky darkened
over New York buildings, the tall street lamps were
lit, innumerable trucks, street cars and elevated trains
clattered by. Nobody and nothing in the great city
stopped for my father's bananas.

"I ought to yell," said my father dolefully. "I
ought to make a big noise like other peddlers, but it

makes my throat sore. Anyway, I'm ashamed of yelling, it makes me feel like a fool."

I had eaten one of his bananas. My sick conscience told me that I ought to pay for it somehow. I must remain here and help my father.

"I'll yell for you, pop," I volunteered.

"Ach, no," he said, "go home; you have worked enough to-day. Just tell momma I'll be late."

But I yelled and yelled. My father, standing by, spoke occasional words of praise, and said I was a wonderful yeller. Nobody else paid attention. The workers drifted past us wearily, endlessly; a defeated army wrapped in dreams of home. Elevated trains crashed; the Cooper Union clock burned above us; the sky grew black, the wind poured, the slush burned through our shoes. There were thousands of strange, silent figures pouring over the sidewalks in snow. None of them stopped to buy bananas. I yelled and yelled, nobody listened.

My father tried to stop me at last. "*Nu,*" he said smiling to console me, "that was wonderful yelling, Mikey. But it's plain we are unlucky to-day! Let's go home."

I was frantic, and almost in tears. I insisted on keeping up my desperate yells. But at last my father persuaded me to leave with him. It was after nightfall. We covered the bananas with an oilcloth and started for the pushcart stable. Down Second Avenue

we plodded side by side. For many blocks my father
was thoughtful. Then he shook his head and sighed:

"So you see how it is, Mikey. Even at banana peddling I am a failure. What can be wrong? The bananas
are good, your yelling was good, the prices are good.
Yes, it is plain; I am a man without luck."

He paused to light his pipe, while I pushed the cart
for him. Then he took the handles again and continued
his meditations.

"Look at me," he said. "Twenty years in America,
and poorer than when I came. A suspender shop I had,
and it was stolen from me by a villain. A house
painter foreman I became, and fell off a scaffold.
Now bananas I sell, and even at that I am a failure.
It is all luck." He sighed and puffed at his pipe.

"Ach, Gott, what a rich country America is! What
an easy place to make one's fortune! Look at all the
rich Jews! Why has it been so easy for them, so hard
for me? I am just a poor little Jew without money."

"Poppa, lots of Jews have no money," I said to
comfort him.

"I know it, my son," he said, "but don't be one of
them. It's better to be dead in this country than not
to have money. Promise me you'll be rich when you
grow up, Mikey!"

"Yes, poppa."

"Ach," he said fondly, "this is my one hope now!
This is all that makes me happy! I am a greenhorn,

but you are an American! You will have it easier than I; you will have luck in America!"

"Yes, poppa," I said, trying to smile with him. But I felt older than he; I could not share his naïve optimism; my heart sank as I remembered the past and thought of the future.

CHAPTER 22

THE JOB HUNT

1

A T the age of twelve I carried in my mind a morbid load of responsibility.

I had been a precocious pupil in the public school, winning honors not by study, but by a kind of intuition. I graduated a year sooner than most boys. At the exercises I was valedictory orator.

My parents were proud, of course. They wanted me to go on to high school, like other "smart" boys. They still believed I would be a doctor.

But I was morbid enough to be wiser than my parents. Even then I could sense that education is a luxury reserved for the well-to-do. I refused to go to high school. More than half the boys in my graduating class were going to work; I chose to be one of them.

It was where I belonged. I figured it out on paper for my parents. Four years of high school, then six years of college before one could be a doctor. Ten years of study in all, with thousands of dollars needed for books, tuition, and the rest.

There were four of us in my family. My mother seemed unable to work. Would my father's banana peddling keep us alive during those ten years while I was studying?

Of course not. I was obstinate and bitter; my parents wept, and tried to persuade me, but I refused to go to high school.

Miss Barry, the English teacher, tried to persuade me, too. She was fond of me. She stared at me out of wistful blue eyes, with her old maid's earnestness, and said:

"It would be a pity for you to go into a factory. I have never seen better English compositions than yours, Michael."

"I must work, Miss Barry," I said. I started to leave. She took my hand. I could smell the fresh spring lilacs in the brass bowl on her desk.

"Wait," she said earnestly, "I want you to promise me to study at night. I will give you a list of the required high school reading; you can make up your Regents' counts that way. Will you do it?"

"Yes, Miss Barry," I lied to her sullenly.

I was trying to be hard. For years my ego had been fed by every one's praise of my precocity. I had always loved books; I was mad about books; I wanted passionately to go to high school and college. Since I couldn't, I meant to despise all that nonsense.

"It will be difficult to study at night," said Miss Barry in her trembly voice, "but Abraham Lincoln did it, and other great Americans."

"Yes, Miss Barry," I muttered.

She presented me with a parting gift. It was a

volume of Emerson's Essays, with her name and my name and the date written on the flyleaf.

I thanked her for the book, and threw it under the bed when I got home. I never read a page in it, or in any book for the next five years. I hated books; they were lies, they had nothing to do with life and work.

It was not easy to find my first job. I hunted for months, in a New York summer of furnace skies and fogs of humidity. I bought the *World* each morning, and ran through the want ads:

Agents Wanted—Addressers Wanted—Barbers Wanted—Bushelmen Wanted—Butchers Wanted—Boys Wanted—

That fateful ad page bringing news of life and death each morning to hundreds of thousands. How often have I read it with gloomy heart. Even to-day the sight of it brings back the ache and hopelessness of my youth.

There was a swarm of boys pushing and yapping like homeless curs at the door of each job. I competed with them. We scrambled, flunkeyed and stood at servile attention under the boss's eye, little slaves on the block.

No one can go through the shame and humiliation of the job-hunt without being marked for life. I hated my first experience at it, and have hated every other since. There can be no freedom in the world while men must beg for jobs.

I rose at six-thirty each morning, and was out tramping the streets at seven. There were always hundreds of jobs, but thousands of boys clutching after them. The city was swarming with these boys, aimless, bewildered and as hungry for work as I was.

I found a job as errand boy in a silk house. But it was temporary. The very first morning the shipping clerk, a refined Nordic, suddenly realized I was a Jew. He politely fired me. They wanted no Jews. In this city of a million Jews, there was much anti-Semitism among business firms. Many of the ads would read: Gentile Only. Even Jewish business houses discriminated against Jews. How often did I slink out of factory or office where a foreman said Jews were not wanted. How often was I made to remember I belonged to the accursed race, the race whose chief misfortune it is to have produced a Christ.

At last I found a job. It was in a factory where incandescent gas mantles were made, a dark loft under the elevated trains on the Bowery near Chatham Square.

This was a spectral place, a chamber of hell, hot and poisoned by hundreds of gas flames. It was suffocating with the stink of chemicals.

I began to sweat immediately. What was worse, I could not breathe. The place terrified me. The boss came up and told me to take off my coat. He was a grim little man, thick as a cask about the middle, and

dressed in a gaudy pink silk shirt. He chewed a cigar.
His face was morbid and hard like a Jewish gangster's.

"Monkey Face," he called, "show this new kid what
to do."

An overgrown Italian boy approached, in pants
and undershirt streaked with sweat. His slit nose, ape
muzzle, and tiny malicious eyes had earned him his
appropriate nickname.

"Come here, kid," he said. I followed him down
the loft. There were thirty unfortunate human beings
at work. Men sat at a long table testing mantles. Their
faces were death masks, fixed and white. Great blue
spectacles shielded their eyes.

Little Jewish and Italian girls dipped racks of
mantles in chemical tanks. Boys stood before a series
of ovens in which sixty gas jets blazed. They passed in
the racks for the chemicals to burn off. Every one
dripped with sweat; every one was haggard, as though
in pain.

"Where did yuh work last?" growled Monkey Face.

"It's my first job. I'm just out of school."

"Yeh?" he snickered. "Just out of school, huh?
Well, yuh struck a good job, kid; it'll put hair on
your chest. Here, take dis."

I took the iron rack he gave me, and dropped it at
once. It scorched my hand. Monkey Face laughed at
the joke.

"You son-of-a-bitch!" I said, "it's hot."

He pushed his apish face close to mine.

"Yuh little kike, I'll bite your nose off if yuh get fresh wit' me! I'm your boss around here."

He went away. I worked. Racks of mantles were brought me, and I burned them off. Hell flamed and stank around me. At noon the boss blew a whistle. We sat on benches for our half-hour lunch. I could not eat for nausea. I wanted air, air, but there was no time for air.

There was no time for anything but work in that evil hell-hole. I sweated there for six months. Monkey Face tortured me. I lost fifteen pounds in weight. I raged in nightmares in my sleep. I forgot my college dreams; I forgot everything, but the gas mantles.

My mother saw how thin I was becoming. She forced me to quit that job. I was too stupefied to have done this myself. Then I read the Want Ads for another month. I found a job in a dark Second Avenue rat-hole, a little printing shop. Here I worked for another five months until I injured my hand in a press.

Another spell of job-hunting. Then a brief interval in a matzoth bakery. Job in an express company. Job in a mail order house. Job in a dry goods store.

Jobs, jobs. I drifted from one to the other, without plan, without hope. I was one of the many. I was caught like my father in poverty's trap. I was nothing, bound for nowhere.

At times I seriously thought of cutting my throat. At other times I dreamed of running away to the far west. Sex began to torture me. I developed a crazy religious streak. I prayed on the tenement roof in moonlight to the Jewish Messiah who would redeem the world. I took up with Nigger again. I spent my nights in a tough poolroom. I needed desperate stimulants; I was ready for anything. At the age of fifteen I began drinking and whoring with Nigger's crowd.

And I worked. And my father and mother grew sadder and older. It went on for years. I don't want to remember it all; the years of my adolescence. Yet I was only one among a million others.

A man on an East Side soap-box, one night, proclaimed that out of the despair, melancholy and helpless rage of millions, a world movement had been born to abolish poverty.

I listened to him.

O workers' Revolution, you brought hope to me, a lonely, suicidal boy. You are the true Messiah. You will destroy the East Side when you come, and build there a garden for the human spirit.

O Revolution, that forced me to think, to struggle and to live.

O great Beginning!

THE END

FINE WORKS OF FICTION
AVAILABLE IN QUALITY
PAPERBACK EDITIONS FROM
CARROLL & GRAF

☐ Asch, Sholem/THE NAZARENE	$10.95
☐ Asch, Sholem/THREE CITIES	$10.50
☐ Balzac, Honoré de/CESAR BIROTTEAU	$8.95
☐ Balzac, Honoré de/THE LILY OF THE VALLEY	$9.95
☐ Bellaman, Henry/KINGS ROW	$8.95
☐ Bernanos, George/DIARY OF A COUNTRY PRIEST	$7.95
☐ Brand, Christianna/GREEN FOR DANGER	$8.95
☐ Chekov, Anton/LATE BLOOMING FLOWERS	$8.95
☐ Conrad, Joseph/EASTERN SKIES, WESTERN SEAS	$12.95
☐ Conrad, Joseph/SEA STORIES	$8.95
☐ Conrad, Joseph & Ford Madox Ford/ ROMANCE	$8.95
☐ Cozzens James Gould/THE LAST ADAM	$8.95
☐ Dalby, Richard/VICTORIAN GHOST STORIES	$9.95
☐ Delbanco, Nicholas/GROUP PORTRAIT	$10.95
☐ de Maupassant, Guy/THE DARK SIDE	$8.95
☐ Dos Passos, John/THREE SOLDIERS	$9.95
☐ Durrell, Laurence/THE BLACK BOOK	$8.95
☐ Feuchtwanger, Lion/JEW SUSS	$8.95
☐ Feuchtwanger, Lion/THE OPPERMANNS	$8.95
☐ Fitzgerald, Penelope/THE BEGINNING OF SPRING	$8.95
☐ Fitzgerald, Penelope/INNOCENCE	$7.95
☐ Fitzgerald, Penelope/OFFSHORE	$7.95
☐ Flaubert, Gustave/NOVEMBER	$7.95
☐ Forster, E.M./GREAT NOVELS OF E.M. FORSTER	$13.95
☐ Fuchs, Daniel/SUMMER IN WILLIAMSBURG	$8.95
☐ Gold, Michael/JEWS WITHOUT MONEY	$7.95
☐ Gorky, Maxim/THE LIFE OF A USELESS MAN	$10.95
☐ Greenberg & Waugh (eds.)/THE NEW ADVENTURES OF SHERLOCK HOLMES	$8.95
☐ Greenfeld, Josh/THE RETURN OF MR. HOLLYWOOD	$8.95
☐ Greene, Graham & Hugh/THE SPY'S BEDSIDE BOOK	$7.95
☐ Hamsun, Knut/MYSTERIES	$8.95
☐ Higgins, George V./TWO COMPLETE NOVELS	$11.95
☐ Hugo, Victor/NINETY-THREE	$8.95
☐ Huxley, Aldous/ANTIC HAY	$10.95
☐ Huxley, Aldous/CROME YELLOW	$10.95
☐ Huxley, Aldous/EYELESS IN GAZA	$9.95
☐ Jackson, Charles/THE LOST WEEKEND	$7.95
☐ James, Henry/GREAT SHORT NOVELS	$11.95
☐ Just, Ward/THE CONGRESSMAN WHO LOVED FLAUBERT	$8.95
☐ Lewis, Norman/DAY OF THE FOX	$8.95
☐ Lowry, Malcolm/ULTRAMARINE	$7.95
☐ Macaulay, Rose/CREWE TRAIN	$8.95
☐ Macaulay, Rose/DANGEROUS AGES	$8.95

☐ Mailer, Norman/BARBARY SHORE $9.95
☐ Maugham, W. Somerset/THE EXPLORER $10.95
☐ Mauriac, François/VIPER'S TANGLE $8.95
☐ Mauriac, François/THE DESERT OF LOVE $6.95
☐ Mauriac, François/FLESH AND BLOOD $8.95
☐ McElroy, Joseph/LOOKOUT CARTRIDGE $9.95
☐ McElroy, Joseph/THE LETTER LEFT TO ME $6.95
☐ McElroy, Joseph/A SMUGGLER'S BIBLE $9.50
☐ Mitford, Nancy/DON'T TELL ALFRED $7.95
☐ Moorcock, Michael/THE BROTHEL IN ROSENSTRASSE $6.95
☐ Munro, H.H./THE NOVELS AND PLAYS OF SAKI $8.95
☐ Neider, Charles (ed.)/GREAT SHORT STORIES $11.95
☐ Neider, Charles (ed.)/SHORT NOVELS
    OF THE MASTERS $12.95
☐ O'Faolain, Julia/THE OBEDIENT WIFE $7.95
☐ O'Faolain, Julia/NO COUNTRY FOR YOUNG MEN $8.95
☐ O'Faolain, Julia/WOMEN IN THE WALL $8.95
☐ Olinto, Antonio/THE WATER HOUSE $8.95
☐ O'Mara, Lesley/GREAT CAT TALES $9.95
☐ Pronzini & Greenberg (eds.)/THE MAMMOTH BOOK OF
    PRIVATE EYE NOVELS $8.95
☐ Rechy, John/BODIES AND SOULS $8.95
☐ Rechy, John/MARILYN'S DAUGHTER $8.95
☐ Rhys, Jean/AFTER LEAVING MR. MACKENZIE $8.95
☐ Rhys, Jean/QUARTET $7.95
☐ Sand, George/MARIANNE $7.95
☐ Scott, Evelyn/THE WAVE $9.95
☐ Singer, I.J./THE BROTHERS ASHKENAZI $9.95
☐ Taylor, Elizabeth/IN A SUMMER SEASON $8.95
☐ Thornton, Louise et al./TOUCHING FIRE $9.95
☐ Tolstoy, Leo/TALES OF COURAGE AND CONFLICT $11.95
☐ Wassermann, Jacob/CASPAR HAUSER $9.95
☐ Weldon, Fay/LETTERS TO ALICE $6.95
☐ Werfel, Franz/THE FORTY DAYS OF MUSA DAGH $13.95
☐ West, Rebecca/THE RETURN OF THE SOLDIER $8.95